Matthew tells us the Good News about Jesus

Bible Society

Bible Society
Trinity Business Centre
Stonehill Green, Westlea
Swindon SN5 7DG
biblesociety.org.uk
bibleresources.org.uk

EasyEnglish Bible translation, copyright © 1997–2010 MissionAssist,
previously known as Wycliffe Associates (UK). This publication is in EasyEnglish
Level A (1200 words).

For permission to use excerpts of the EasyEnglish Bible translation please
contact MissionAssist, PO Box 257, Evesham WR11 9AW
Charity registration number 1007772
Visit: easyenglish.info

EasyEnglish Gospel of Matthew
ISBN 978 0 564 04953 0

Typography and typesetting by Bible Society Resources Ltd,
a wholly-owned subsidiary of The British and Foreign Bible Society
Cover design by Patrick Knowles
Production arranged by Bible Society Resources Ltd

EEGMAT/BSRL/2022/0.25M
Printed in the United Kingdom

CONTENTS

Matthew tells us the Good News about Jesus 1

Matthew 3

Word List 111

Matthew tells us the Good News about Jesus

This is about the book that Matthew wrote

A man called Matthew wrote this book at some time between the years AD* 59 and AD* 70. Matthew was a Jew* and he was sometimes called Levi. He received taxes* for the government before he became a disciple* of Jesus. He may have written his book when he was living in Israel*. But he may have written it when he was living in Antioch. Antioch is a city in the country called Syria. Matthew wrote the book in the Greek* language. He wrote it for Jews* who understood Greek*. In his book, Matthew wrote many things about the messages that God's prophets* had written a long time ago. The Jews* who read Matthew's book would know all about these things.

Matthew tells us the Good News about the Kingdom* of God. He tells us about the birth of Jesus and how he lived. He tells us how Jesus died. He tells us how he went to live with God again. He also tells us who Jesus is. And he tells us why he came to live in the world. Matthew explained the things that Jesus taught the people. And he tells us about many things that Jesus did.

The Jews* were waiting for God to send a special person to them. They called this person the Messiah. God had promised to send him. It means the person whom God sent to save people from punishment*. He would also be the king of the Jews*. He is the only person who can put us right with God. In the Greek* language, the special person was called Christ.

Matthew knew that Jesus was that special person. He wanted other people also to know this.

Matthew wrote his book in 8 parts:

1:1 – 2:23 what happened when Jesus was born.

3:1 – 4:11 what happened when Jesus began his work.

4:12 – 14:12 what happened when Jesus was working in Galilee.

14:13 – 17:21 what happened when Jesus went to other places in the north of Israel*.

17:22 – 18:35 what happened when Jesus returned to Galilee.

19:1 - 20:34 what happened when Jesus taught the people in Judea and Perea.

21:1 – 27:66 what happened in the city called Jerusalem in the last week of Jesus' life.

28:1 – 28:20 people see Jesus alive again after he died.

(Galilee, Judea and Perea were all different parts of the country called Israel*.)

MATTHEW

1

The ancestors* of Jesus

¹These are the names of people in the family of Jesus Christ. Jesus was in the family of King David. David was in the family of Abraham.

²Abraham was the father of Isaac.
Isaac was the father of Jacob.
Jacob was the father of Judah and his brothers.
³Judah was the father of Perez and Zerah. Their mother was called Tamar.
Perez was the father of Hezron.
Hezron was the father of Ram.
⁴Ram was the father of Amminadab.
Amminadab was the father of Nahshon.
Nahshon was the father of Salmon.
⁵Salmon was the father of Boaz (his mother was called Rahab).
Boaz was the father of Obed (his mother was called Ruth).
Obed was the father of Jesse.
⁶Jesse was the father of King David.
David was Solomon's father. Solomon's mother was the wife of Uriah.
⁷Solomon was the father of Rehoboam.
Rehoboam was the father of Abijah.
Abijah was the father of Asa.
⁸Asa was the father of Jehoshaphat.
Jehoshaphat was the father of Jehoram.
Jehoram was the father of Uzziah.

9Uzziah was the father of Jotham.
Jotham was the father of Ahaz.
Ahaz was the father of Hezekiah.
10Hezekiah was the father of Manasseh.
Manasseh was the father of Amon.
Amon was the father of Josiah.
Josiah was the father of Jeconiah and his brothers.

11This was when soldiers from Babylon took the Jews* away
to Babylon.

12Here is a list of the people who lived after that time:

Jeconiah was the father of Shealtiel.
Shealtiel was the father of Zerubbabel.
13Zerubbabel was the father of Abiud.
Abiud was the father of Eliakim.
Eliakim was the father of Azor.
14Azor was the father of Zadok.
Zadok was the father of Akim.
Akim was the father of Eliud.
15Eliud was the father of Eleazar.
Eleazar was the father of Matthan.
Matthan was the father of Jacob.
16Jacob was the father of Joseph.

Joseph married Mary. Mary was the mother of Jesus Christ.
Jesus was the special person that God sent to save his people.

17So then, there were 14 generations from Abraham to David.
There were 14 generations from David to the time the Jews*
went to Babylon. There were 14 generations from then until
Jesus was born.

Jesus is born

18Now this is how Jesus Christ was born. His mother's name
was Mary. She had promised to marry a man called Joseph.
Then she discovered that a baby was growing inside her. This
happened before she married Joseph. The powerful Holy

Spirit* had caused this to happen to her. [19]Joseph always wanted to do what was right. He did not want everyone to know about Mary's baby. He did not want her to be ashamed. So he had a plan to stop the marriage secretly.

[20]Joseph thought about what to do. Then an angel* came from God to see him. While he was dreaming, the angel* said, 'Joseph, you who are from the family of King David, do not be afraid to take Mary as your wife. The baby that is growing inside her is from God's Holy Spirit*. [21]Mary's baby will be a boy. He will save his people from the wrong things that they have done. Because of this, you must name him Jesus.'

[22]Many years before, God had spoken to one of his prophets* about this. Now God's words would soon become true. The prophet* called Isaiah had said, [23]'There will be a young woman who has never had sex. A baby boy will grow inside her. People will call him Immanuel . This name means "God is with us".'

[24]Then Joseph woke up from his sleep. He did what God's angel* had asked him to do. He married Mary. [25]Joseph did not have sex with Mary before the baby boy was born. Joseph said that the baby should be called Jesus.

2

Some men come to visit Jesus

[1]Jesus was born in the town called Bethlehem in Judea. At that time, King Herod ruled Judea. Soon after Jesus was born, some clever men came from the east to Jerusalem.

[2]The men arrived in Jerusalem and they asked people, 'Where is the baby who was born a short time ago as the King of the Jews*? We ask because we saw a special star. This star rose in the east. We knew about the baby king when we saw this star. We want to bend our knees in front of him. We want to tell him how great and important he is.'

3 Herod heard what the men were saying. And he became anxious*. Many people in Jerusalem were also anxious*. 4 Then Herod asked all the leaders of the priests* and the teachers of the Law* to meet with him. He asked them, 'God promised to send a special person. Where will that special person be born?' 5 Then the leaders of the priests* and the teachers of the Law* replied, 'The special person will be born in Bethlehem in Judea. This is what the prophet* wrote about Bethlehem.

6 "God said:

> People in Bethlehem,
> your town is one of the most important towns in Judea.
> A person born in your town will rule my people Israel*. He
>   will guide my people." '

7 Herod listened to all these things. So he asked the visitors to meet with him by himself. Herod asked them some questions. And he discovered the time that the star had appeared. 8 Then Herod sent the men to Bethlehem. 'Go and look everywhere for this child', he said. 'And when you find him, come back here. Then you can tell me where he is. After that, I can also bend my knees in front of him. I can tell him how great and important he is.'

9 After the men had heard the king, they continued their journey. While they were travelling, the same star appeared again. 10 The star moved along in front of them. Then it stopped above the place where the child was staying. The men were very happy when they saw the star. 11 They went into the house and they saw the child. He was with Mary, his mother. They went down on their knees in front of the child. They said to him, 'You are very great and important.' Then they opened their bags. They took out valuable gifts and they gave them to the child. The gifts were gold, incense called frankincense and myrrh. 12 God said to them in a dream, 'Do not go back to see Herod.' So the men returned to their own country by a different road.

Mary, Joseph and Jesus go to Egypt

13 That night, after the men had gone away, Joseph had a dream. He saw one of God's angels* who said to him, 'Herod will be looking for the child, so that his soldiers can kill him. You must get up and take the child and his mother with you. Go immediately to the country called Egypt. You will all be safe there. I will tell you when you can leave. You must remain there until then.'

14 So Joseph got up and he took the child and the child's mother with him. They started on the journey to Egypt that same night. 15 They all remained in Egypt until Herod died. This happened to cause the words of the prophet* to become true. God had said by the prophet*, 'I have brought my son out of Egypt.'

Herod's soldiers kill the baby boys in Bethlehem

16 Then Herod understood that his visitors from the east would not return to him. He was very angry. He sent his soldiers to Bethlehem. He said to them, 'Kill all the baby boys in Bethlehem. Kill those boys also who live near there. Kill all those who are not more than 2 years old.' The visitors had told Herod that they had first seen the star 2 years ago. So he chose to kill the baby boys of that age. 17 In this way, the words that Jeremiah the prophet* spoke became true.

18 He had said,

'People heard a noise in the town called Ramah.
They heard someone weeping with a loud voice.
It is Rachel and she is crying for her children.
Her children are dead,
So nobody can help her to feel better.'

Joseph, Mary and Jesus return to Israel* from Egypt

¹⁹After Herod died, Joseph saw one of God's angels* in a dream. ²⁰'Get up', said the angel*. 'The people who wanted to kill the child are dead. Take the child and his mother. You can return with them to Israel*.'

²¹So Joseph got up. He took the child and the child's mother and they travelled to Israel*. ²²But then, Joseph heard that Archelaus, Herod's son, was now king of Judea. So Joseph was afraid to go to Judea. Joseph had another dream. An angel* explained to him what to do. 'Go to Galilee instead', he said. ²³Joseph made his home in a town called Nazareth. So what the prophets* had said became true. 'He will be called a person from Nazareth.'

3

John the Baptist* prepares a way for Jesus

¹Some years later, a man called John the Baptist* went to the desert* in Judea. He began to tell people a message from God.

²John said, 'Stop doing wrong things. Say sorry to God and obey him. You must do this because the Kingdom* of heaven is coming soon.'

³John the Baptist* is the man that the prophet* Isaiah spoke about. Isaiah said,

> 'You will hear someone shouting in the desert* these words:
> "The LORD is coming, so prepare a road for him to travel on.
> Make the path straight." '

⁴ Now John always wore a coat that he had made out of hair from a camel. He also wore a leather belt. His usual food was large insects and honey from the desert*.

⁵ Many of the people went to listen to John. They lived in Jerusalem and Judea and all the other places near the river

Jordan. ⁶The people told God about all the wrong things
that they had done. Then John baptised* the people in the
river Jordan.

⁷Many Pharisees* and Sadducees* came to John. They
wanted John to baptise* them. He said to them, 'You are
like dangerous snakes. You are trying to run away from God
because he is angry with you. He will soon punish* people who
do wrong things. ⁸Stop doing the things that God does not
like. Do things to show God that you are sorry. ⁹Do not say to
yourselves, "We are in the family of Abraham. So God will not
punish* us." Listen! God can make children for Abraham out of
these stones! ¹⁰You are like trees. God has an axe ready at the
lowest part of the trees. He will cut down every tree that does
not make good fruit. He will throw these trees into the fire.'

¹¹'I baptise* you with water. This shows God that you are
sorry. You are sorry about the wrong things that you have
done. It shows him that you now want to obey his rules. But a
person is coming soon. He is more important than I am. I am
not at all good like he is. I am no good even to carry his shoes
for him. He will baptise* you with the Holy Spirit* and he will
baptise* you with fire. ¹²He is like a farmer with a special tool
in his hand. A farmer throws the wheat* up in the air with this
tool. He does this to remove the dry hard part that is outside
of the seed. He cannot use this hard part for anything, so he
burns it in a fire. Nobody can put out this fire. But he will put
the seeds in a building to keep them safe.'

John baptises* Jesus

¹³Then Jesus came from Galilee to the river Jordan. He
wanted John to baptise* him. ¹⁴But John did not want to
baptise* Jesus. He said to Jesus, 'I should come to you instead,
and then you can baptise* me. But you are asking me to
baptise* you.'

15 Jesus replied, 'This time, do what I ask you. God wants you to baptise* me. And we must do everything that is proper.' So John did what Jesus asked him to do.

16 When John baptised* him, Jesus came up out of the water. Then God opened the sky and Jesus saw God's Spirit coming down. He came down like a bird, which sat on Jesus. 17 Then Jesus heard a voice in the sky. 'This man is my Son. I love him and he makes me very happy.'

4

The devil* tries to cause Jesus to do wrong things

1 God's Spirit led Jesus into the desert*. Here the devil* tried to cause Jesus to do wrong things.

2 Jesus did not eat anything for 40 days and 40 nights. He was very hungry at the end of this time. 3 Then the devil* came to Jesus and said to him, 'If you are the Son of God, you can talk to these stones. Tell the stones that they must become bread.'

4 But Jesus answered the devil*, 'Moses wrote this in God's book. "People need more than bread to really live. They need to hear every word that God speaks. Then they can really live." '

5 Then the devil* led Jesus to Jerusalem. He took Jesus to stand on the highest point of God's Great House. 6 He said to Jesus, 'If you are God's Son, jump down from here to the ground. Someone wrote in God's book,

> "God will ask his angels* to take care* of you.
> They will hold you in their hands while you fall. And so you
>   will be safe.
> They will not even let you hurt your feet on a stone".'

7 Jesus answered the devil*, 'Moses also wrote in God's book. "You must not do something dangerous to see if God will save you".'

8 Then the devil* led Jesus up a very high mountain. He showed Jesus all the countries in the whole world. They were all very great and beautiful. 9 'I will give you everything that you can see', said the devil*. 'Go down on your knees in front of me. Say that I am great and important and beautiful. And I will give it all to you.'

10 Jesus then said to him, 'Go away. Moses also wrote this in God's book. "We must only go down on our knees in front of God. We must only tell him, 'You are great and important'. We must obey him first".'

11 Then the devil* left Jesus alone. After that, angels* came to Jesus and they took care* of him.

Jesus starts his work in Galilee

12 Now Jesus heard that Herod's soldiers had put John the Baptist* in prison. So Jesus returned to Galilee.

13 He did not stay in Nazareth. He went to live in a town called Capernaum. Capernaum is on the shore of Lake Galilee. It was in the part of Israel* called Zebulun and Naphtali.

14 Jesus went to live in Capernaum. And this caused the words of God to become true. God had said this to his prophet* who was called Isaiah.

15 'I am speaking to you people who live in Zebulun and
    Naphtali.
   Your part of this country is on the way to Lake Galilee.
   It is across the River Jordan in the part of the country
    called Galilee.
   Some people who are not Jews* live there.
16 They are like people who are living in the dark.
   They live in the shadow which death brings.
   God will send a light to shine on them.'

17 Then Jesus began to teach the people. 'Stop doing wrong things. Say to God that you are sorry', Jesus said. 'Begin

to obey God. You must do all this because the Kingdom* of Heaven* is coming soon.'

Jesus asks some men to be his disciples*

18 One day, Jesus was walking along the shore of Lake Galilee. He saw two men. One man was called Simon, and he was also called Peter. The other man's name was Andrew, and he was Simon's brother. Their job was to catch fish. They were throwing their nets* into the lake to catch some fish. 19 'Come with me and be my disciples*', Jesus said to them. 'And I will teach you how to catch people.'

20 Peter and Andrew immediately stopped working with their nets*. They went with Jesus and they became his disciples*.

21 Then Jesus continued to walk along the shore of Lake Galilee. Soon he saw two more men. Their job also was to catch fish. They were called James and John. They were brothers and their father was called Zebedee. John, James and Zebedee were in their boat and they were mending their nets*. Jesus said to James and John, 'Come with me and be my disciples*.' 22 Then the brothers immediately left the boat and their father behind. They went with Jesus and they became his disciples*.

Jesus teaches the people about God and he makes sick people well again

23 Jesus went everywhere in Galilee. He went into the building where the Jews* met to pray. Then he taught the people the good news about the Kingdom*. People who had many different illnesses and problems came to Jesus. He caused all these people to become well again. 24 So people began to hear about Jesus more and more. People in Syria also heard about Jesus, so they brought all the sick people to see him. They wanted Jesus to cause them to become well again. They had many different illnesses and some had pains. Bad spirits* were living inside some of them. Some people had sick minds, and some people could not move. Jesus caused all these people to

become well again. ²⁵Because of this, large crowds followed him. These people came from Galilee and the Decapolis, and from Jerusalem. They also came from the part of Judea that is on the other side of the River Jordan.

5

Jesus teaches those who followed him

¹Jesus saw all the crowds following him. So he went up a hill and he sat down there to teach. Jesus' disciples* went close to listen to him. ²And he began to teach them.

³'Some people', he said, 'know that they need God very much. God will cause those people to be happy because they will be part of the Kingdom* of Heaven*.

⁴Some people are sad now. God will help them to feel better. They will be happy.'

⁵'Some people know that they are not powerful. They will be happy. God will give them what he has promised them.

⁶Some people want to obey God more than they want to do anything else. God will give to them all that they need.

⁷Some people are kind and they forgive* other people. They will be happy. God will be kind to them and he will forgive* them.

⁸Some people do not want to do wrong things. They will be happy because they will see God.

⁹Some people help other people to be friends and to agree together. They will be happy because God will call them his children.

¹⁰Some people will have pain because they obey God. They will be happy because they are part of the Kingdom* of Heaven*.

11 You will be happy when people say bad things about you. Sometimes people will hurt you. Sometimes people will say things about you that are not true. People will do these things to you because you are my disciples*. 12 You should be very happy when people do these things to any of you. You should shout because you are so happy. God has kept many good things for you. He will give you these things when you go to heaven*. People did all these same things to the prophets* who lived a long time ago.'

Jesus' disciples* are like salt and light

13 'You are like salt', Jesus said, 'for all people to taste and use. Salt is good. But sometimes it does not taste like salt any longer. That salt cannot become good again. It is not good for people to use for anything. They throw it outside and they walk on it.

14 You are like the light that everybody needs in this world. If people build a city on a hill, then other people can see it easily. 15 Nobody lights a lamp* and then puts it under a can. He will put the lamp* in a high place. Everybody who is in the house can then see the light from the lamp*. 16 You must be sure that you shine like that light. Then everybody will be able to see. People will see all the lovely things that you do. Then they will say good things about God. He is your Father in heaven*.'

Jesus talks about the Laws* that Moses gave to the Jews*

17 Jesus said, 'You should not think that I have come to destroy the Law*. Also, I have not come to destroy the messages that the prophets* wrote down. No, I have not come to destroy their words. I have come to cause what they taught to become true. 18 Remember my words. The sky and the earth will remain for a long time. While they remain, the Law* will also remain. Not even a small change in the Law* will happen. When everything in it has happened, then the Law* will finish. 19 So then a person may think to himself, "This rule is not very important. I will not obey it." He may also teach other

people to think like that. But this teacher will be the least important person in the Kingdom* of Heaven*. On the other hand, a person who obeys all God's rules will be important. He teaches other people also to obey, so he will be great in God's Kingdom*. 20 I am telling you this. You will be able to come into the Kingdom* of Heaven* if you obey him. But you must obey him better than the teachers of the Law* and the Pharisees* do.'

Jesus teaches about angry people

21 'You have heard the words to your people long ago. "You must not kill another person. And any person who does kill will stand in front of a judge*. This judge* will say that he has done something wrong. And he will punish* him." 22 But now, I say this to you about it. Anybody who is angry with his brother without a good reason will stand in front of a judge*. The judge* may say that this angry person has done a wrong thing. Someone might call his brother by a bad name. Then, the most important rulers will judge* him. They may say that he must be punished*. But whoever says, "You are a fool", to their brother, God will judge* him. He may say to him, "You should go into the fire in hell*." '

23 'Maybe you go to give your gift to God', said Jesus to them. 'You take it to the special table in God's Great House. But then you remember that your brother is angry with you. 24 You must leave your gift there in front of God's special table. And you must first go and find your brother. Say to him that you are sorry. Then you can both become friends with each other again. After that, you can go back and give your gift to God.

25 A person may say that you have done something wrong. So he will take you to stand in front of the judge*. You should try to agree with this person. You should decide with him what is right. Do this even while you are going with him to the judge*. Do it so that he will not speak against you to the judge*. The judge* may agree with him that you have done a wrong thing. Then he will give you to his officer who will put you in prison.

26 What I say is true. You will remain in prison until you have paid all the money.'

Jesus teaches people about not doing wrong things

27 'You know what God said to your people long ago. "You must not have sex with a person who is not your husband or wife. If you do, then you have done a wrong thing." 28 But I tell you this. A man looks at a woman who is not his wife. And he wants to have sex with her. Now this man has also done a wrong thing. 29 If your right eye makes you do wrong things, then you should take it out. You should throw it away. You will lose one eye. But it will be much worse if God throws you with your two eyes into hell*. 30 If your right hand makes you do wrong things, then you should cut it off. You should throw it away. You will lose one hand. But it is much worse if God sends you with your two hands into hell*.'

Jesus talks about when a man sends his wife away

31 'These words are also in God's Law*. "Any man who wants to stop being married to his wife must give her a paper. This paper shows that they are now separate." 32 But now, I tell you this. A man must only become separate from his wife because of one reason. This reason is that his wife has had sex with another man. If his wife has not done this, then she is still his wife. The paper does not cause the man and his wife to be separate. Now, if his wife marries another man she is doing a wrong thing. And the other man who marries her is also doing a wrong thing.'

Jesus teaches people about promises to God

33 'You know what God also said to your people long ago. "If you make a promise to God and use his name, do what you have said." 34 But I tell you this. Do not use God's name to make a promise. Do not use the words "by heaven*" to make a promise. Heaven* is the place where God rules. Do not use the words "by the earth" to make a promise. The earth is the

place where God rests his feet. 35 Do not use the words "by Jerusalem" to make a promise. Jerusalem is God's city. He is the great King there. 36 Do not use the words "my head" to make a promise. You cannot make the colour of your hair black or white. 37 You should say only "Yes" if you mean, "Yes, I will do it." And you should say only "No" if you mean, "No, I will not do it." If you say more than this, what you say comes from the Devil*.'

Jesus teaches them about how to love people

38 'So, this is also in God's Law*. "If a man destroys somebody's eye, then somebody should destroy that man's eye. If a man destroys a man's tooth, then somebody should destroy that man's tooth." 39 But I tell you this. If somebody does something bad to you, do not try to do something bad back to him. Somebody may slap you on one side of your face. Then you should let him slap you on the other side of your face also.'

40 'Maybe somebody wants to take you to the judge*. He says to the judge*, "This man has done a wrong thing against me. So I want him to give me his shirt." Give the man your shirt. Give him also your coat. 41 A soldier may say to you, "Carry my luggage for one mile (1500 metres)." Help him. Carry it for two miles (3000 metres). 42 When somebody asks you for something, you should give it to him. If somebody asks you to lend him something, then you should not refuse.

43 You hear people say, "Love the people who are your friends. Do not love those who want to hurt you." 44 But I tell you this. You should love the people who want to hurt you. Some people hurt you because you obey God. You should pray to God that he would help them. 45 If you do this, you will be sons and daughters of your Father above. He causes the sun to shine on people who obey him. He also causes the sun to shine on people who do not obey him. God causes the rain to fall on people who obey him. He also causes the rain to fall on people who do not obey him. 46 You might only love people who love

you. But then, God will not pay you for doing that. Even men who take the taxes* do it!'

47'When you only speak to your friends', said Jesus, 'then you are not doing anything extra. Even people who do not believe in God do that. 48 So you must be good in every way, as your Father above is good in every way.'

6

Jesus teaches people how to help poor people

1 Jesus still spoke to them. 'You may do good things and help somebody. But be careful that you do not want other people to see you. Let it be a secret. If you do these things to show people, God, your Father in heaven* will not pay you back.

2 When you give something to a poor person, do not tell anyone about it. The hypocrites* do this in the buildings where people meet to pray. They also do it outside in the busy streets of the town. They do this so that other people will say, "These men are good." What I say is true. They have already received good words from other people. So, God will not give them anything more.'

3 'When you give something to a poor person, keep it a secret. Do not tell even your best friend. Let it be as if your left hand did not know about your right hand's actions. 4 Nobody else will know about what you gave to the person. It will be a secret. God sees things that are secret. And he will give you good things.'

Jesus teaches people how to pray

5 'So, you must not pray like the hypocrites* pray. They like to stand and pray in the Jewish* meeting places and on the busy corners of the streets. Then many people can see them praying. What I say is true. They have already received good words from people and they will not get anything more.'

⁶'I will tell you how to pray. Go to a place in your house where you can be alone. There you can pray to God your Father. He is in that secret place. And he sees what you do. He will give you good things. ⁷When you pray, do not say the same words many times. And do not use many words that mean nothing. People who do not believe in God do that. And they think that God will hear them. ⁸Do not be like them. God your Father already knows what you need. He knows this even before you ask him.

⁹This then is how you should pray,

"God our Father, you live in heaven*.
You are powerful and important.
We want more and more people to know that your name
    has great authority.
¹⁰ We want you to rule everyone.
We want everyone to obey you on earth, like everyone in
    heaven* obeys you.
¹¹ Please give us the food that we need each day.
¹² Please forgive* us for all the wrong things that we have
    done.
We have forgiven* everyone who has done wrong things to
    us.
Forgive* us in the same way.
¹³ Do not let anything cause us to do wrong things.
Keep us safe from the Devil*." '

¹⁴Then Jesus said, 'You must forgive* other people for the wrong things that they have done to you. Then God, your Father in heaven* will also forgive* you for the wrong things that you have done to him. ¹⁵But if you do not forgive* other people, then your Father will not forgive* you.'

Jesus teaches the people about how to stop eating for some time

¹⁶'Be careful when you stop eating for some time. Do not look sad. Then people will not know what you are doing. That is what the hypocrites* do. A hypocrite* wants people to think

about how good he is. He will let his face become dirty. Then other people can see that he has stopped eating. You should remember that God will not give the hypocrites* anything else. Other people think that they are good. And that is all that they will get. 17But when you stop eating for some time, you should wash your face. You should cause your hair to look nice. 18Then other people will not know that you have stopped eating for some time. But God your Father knows. He sees what you do in that secret place. So he will give you good things.'

Jesus teaches the people about the valuable things that they have in God's place above

19'Do not have many valuable things here in the world. Here there are insects and water that can destroy them. There are also men who can come into your house. They can rob you of all your valuable things. 20Instead, you should put all your valuable things in God's place above. The insects and water cannot destroy your valuable things there. Men cannot rob you of all your things. 21You will always think about the place where you keep your valuable things. You will want to be there in heaven*.'

22'Eyes are like lamps* and your body is like a room. If your eyes are like a clean lamp*, then your whole body will have light. 23If your eyes are not good, then your whole body will be in the dark. If the light in your body has become dark, you will live in a very dark place.'

Jesus teaches the people about God and the things that we have

24'A slave cannot work for two masters at the same time. He will not like one of the masters, but he will love the other master. He will always say good things about one of the masters and say bad things about the other master. You cannot have God as a master and have money also as your master.'

25 Jesus said to his disciples*, 'What I say is true. Do not be anxious* about food and drink to stay alive. Do not be anxious* about clothes to wear either. Your life is more important than your food, and your body is more important than your clothes. 26 Think about the wild birds. They do not plant seeds in the ground. They do not cut down plants to eat. And they have no buildings to store food. God gives them food. And you are much more valuable than the birds. 27 Perhaps you are anxious* about how long you will live. But you cannot live one hour longer, even if you are always thinking about it. No, you cannot do even a small thing like that. So do not be anxious* about all these other things.

28 You should not be anxious* about your clothes. Think about how the wild flowers grow. They do not work or make clothes for themselves. 29 But this is true. King Solomon wore very beautiful clothes. But even one wild flower is more beautiful than he was. 30 God gives beautiful clothes to the grass and to the wild flowers. They are alive in the field today, but tomorrow people will burn them. God will certainly give you clothes to wear. You should know that God will take care* of you.'

31 Then Jesus said, 'Do not always be thinking about where you will find your food and drink and clothes. Do not be anxious*. 32 People who do not know about God are always thinking about these things. God, your Father in heaven*, knows that you need them. 33 Instead, think about the things that are important in the Kingdom* of God. You should do everything that you can to obey God. Then God will also give you the other things that you need. 34 So do not be anxious* about what might happen tomorrow. Tomorrow there will be enough problems for you to be anxious* about. It is enough for you to be anxious* each day about the problems of that day.'

7

We should not judge* other people

¹Jesus was still speaking to the people. 'Do not say to anybody, "You are a bad person." Then God will not say to you, "You are a bad person." ²God will speak to you in the same way that you speak to other people. He will use the same rules for you as you use for other people.

³Do not look at the small piece of wood dirt that is in your brother's eye. You should first see the big piece of wood that is in your own eye. ⁴You should not say to your brother, "Please let me take the small piece of wood dirt out of your eye." But you yourself have not seen the big piece of wood that is in your own eye. ⁵You think that you are better than your brother. But you are not. First, you must take the big piece of wood out of your own eye. Then your eyes will be clear and you will see well. After that, you can take the small piece of wood dirt out of your brother's eye.'

⁶'Do not give really good things that are for God to dogs. The dogs will turn round and attack you. Do not throw valuable things to pigs. The pigs will only stand on them and bury them in the dirt.'

Jesus teaches his disciples* more about God

⁷'Go on asking God for what you need. And then you will receive. Go on looking for what you need. And then you will find it. Go on knocking at the door. And then God will open it for you. ⁸Everyone who asks for something will receive it. Everyone who looks for something will find it. God will open the door for everyone who knocks on it.

⁹Some of you are fathers. You would not give your son a stone when he asks you for some bread. ¹⁰You would not give your son a snake if he asks you for a fish. ¹¹Even if you are bad, you know how to give good things to your children. Your Father

above knows much better than you do how to give good things. So he will give good things to those people who ask him.'

12 'In the same way that you want other people to do things to you, do things to other people. This is what the Law* of Moses teaches us. It is also what the prophets* wrote in their books.'

Jesus teaches people how to get true life

13 'You should go in through the narrow gate to get true life. The wide gate is easy to go through. The wide path is easy to travel on. Many people find that wide gate, but it is the way to hell*. 14 It is difficult to go through the small gate. It is difficult to walk on the narrow road. But when you do go that way, you will get true life. Not many people find that narrow gate.'

Jesus teaches the story about a tree and its fruit

15 'Watch out for prophets* who tell you wrong things about God. These people seem to be like sheep that are not dangerous. But they are really like hungry wild dogs. What they teach will hurt you.

16 You will know these people by what they do. People do not pick good fruit from weeds. And they do not pick fruit to eat from wild plants.'

17 'Good fruit grows on a tree that is good. Bad fruit grows on a tree that is not good. 18 A good tree cannot make bad fruit. A bad tree cannot make good fruit. 19 The farmer will cut down any tree that does not make good fruit. He will burn that tree on a fire. 20 So you will know if a person is good or bad. Look at what they do. And look at what they say. A good person does good things. And a bad person does bad things.

21 Some people say to me, "Master, Master!" But not all of them will come into the Kingdom* of Heaven*. Only the people who obey God, my Father in heaven*, will come in. They do what he wants them to do. 22 On the day when God judges*, people will say, "Master, Master! We used your authority and

we told people a message from you. We used your authority
and we caused bad spirits* to come out of people. We used
your authority to do many powerful things." 23 Then I will say
to these people, "I never knew you. You do not obey God; you
are bad. So go away from me." '

Jesus tells a story about two men who each built a house

24 'I will tell you about a man. He hears my message and he
obeys it. Now, this person understands my words. He is like
a man who built his house on rock. 25 Then a storm came and
brought a lot of water. The water hit the house and strong
winds blew hard against that house. But the house did not
fall down because the man had built it on rock. 26 Another man
hears my message and he does not obey it. He is like a man
who built his house on sand. 27 Then a storm came and brought
a lot of water. The water hit the house and strong winds blew
hard against it. The house fell down. The storm destroyed
it completely.'

28 Jesus finished speaking. All the people were very surprised
about the things that he taught them. 29 Jesus did not teach
them in the same way as the teachers of the Law*. Jesus had
his own authority when he taught them.

8

A man who had an illness of the
skin comes to meet Jesus

1 A large crowd followed Jesus when he came down from the
hill. 2 Then a man with an illness of the skin came to meet
Jesus. The illness was called leprosy. The man went down on
his knees in front of him. 'Sir, if you want', he said, 'you can
make me well. Please do it.'

3 Jesus put out his hand towards him and touched him. 'I do
want to help you. Be well', he said. Immediately, the illness left
the man. 4 'You must not tell anyone about this', Jesus said to

him. 'Instead, go and show yourself to the priest*. Take him a gift for God, as Moses said. "Do this to thank God for what has happened. And this will also show everyone that you are now well." '

An officer in the army believes that Jesus can help him

5 When Jesus went into Capernaum, an officer in the army came to meet him. He asked Jesus to help him.

6 'Sir, my servant is lying in bed at home. He cannot move and he has a lot of pain.'

7 Jesus said to the officer, 'I will go with you to your house and I will make your servant well again.'

8 But the officer said to Jesus, 'Sir, you are too important to come into my house. You have authority. Instead, you can say that he will be well. And I know that my servant will be well again. 9 Someone has authority over me. I also have authority over other soldiers. I say to this soldier, "Go!" and he goes. I say to that soldier, "Come!" so, he comes. I say to one of my servants, "Do this!" so, he does it.'

10 Jesus heard what the officer said. And Jesus was very surprised. He spoke to the crowd that was following him. 'What I say is true. I have not found anybody like this man in Israel*. Nobody else believes so well in me.'

11 'What I say is true. Many people will come from all over the world. They will take their place in the Kingdom* of Heaven*. They will sit down to eat with Abraham, Isaac and Jacob. 12 Some people were born to belong to the Kingdom*. But God's angels* will throw them into the dark places outside his kingdom*. There the people will cry. And they will bite their teeth together because they are angry.'

13 Then Jesus said to the officer, 'Go home. You believed that I would make your servant well again. So I will do it for you.' And at that moment, Jesus made the servant well again.

Jesus makes many people well again

14 Jesus went into Peter's house. There, he saw the mother of Peter's wife. She was ill in bed and she felt very hot. 15 Jesus touched her hand and immediately she did not feel hot any longer. She got up and she prepared food and drink for Jesus.

16 That evening, some people brought other people to see Jesus. Bad spirits* lived in many of these people. Jesus spoke a word and he caused the bad spirits* to leave them. He made everybody who was ill well again. 17 Jesus did all this to cause the prophet* Isaiah's words to become true:

'He took away all our weaknesses.
He took away everything that makes us sick.'

18 One day, Jesus saw a large crowd round him. So he said to his disciples*, 'Let us cross over to the other side of the lake.' 19 A teacher of the Law* came to Jesus and said to him, 'Teacher, I want to become one of your disciples*. I will go with you everywhere that you go.'

20 Jesus said to him, 'Wild dogs have a place to live. Wild birds also have their own places to live. But the Son of Man has no regular place to lie down and sleep.'

21 Another man who was already a disciple* of Jesus spoke to him. 'Sir, I will come with you. But first, let me go home to bury my father. After that, I will come with you.'

22 Jesus said to him, 'Let those people who are dead bury their own dead people.'

Jesus stops a storm

23 Then Jesus climbed into a boat and his disciples* followed him. 24 A great storm soon started on the lake. Water began to fill the boat, so that soon the boat was almost under the water. Jesus was sleeping. 25 The disciples* went to him and

they woke him. 'Save us, Master', they said. 'We will soon die in the water.'

26 'You should not be so frightened. You do not believe in me very much!' Jesus said. Then he stood up and he spoke to the wind and the water. 'Be quiet!' he said. 'Stop moving!' Then the wind stopped and the water became flat again.

27 The disciples* were very surprised. 'What kind of man is this?' they asked each other. 'Even the wind and the water obey him!'

Jesus makes two men well again

28 Jesus arrived at the other side of Lake Galilee. He was in the part of the country called Gadara. The people who lived there were called Gadarenes. Jesus arrived near the place where they buried dead people. Two men came to meet Jesus. Bad spirits* lived in these two men. The men were very dangerous. Everyone was too afraid to walk near this place because of them. 29 When the two men saw Jesus, they immediately shouted to him, 'What are you going to do with us? You are the Son of God. Have you come to punish* us before the right time?'

30 A large group of pigs was feeding near to this place. 31 The bad spirits* asked Jesus, 'If you cause us to leave these men, please send us to those pigs. Let us go into them.'

32 'Go!' said Jesus to the bad spirits*. So the bad spirits* came out of the men and went into the pigs. All the pigs rushed down the hill. They ran into the lake and they all died in the water. 33 There were some men there, who took care* of the pigs. Those men ran away into the town, when this happened. They told people there everything that had happened to the men with bad spirits*. 34 So everybody came out of the town to meet Jesus. And when they saw him, they said, 'Please leave our part of the country.

9

Jesus helps a man who cannot walk

1 Jesus then climbed back into the boat and he sailed across to the other side of the lake again. He returned to Capernaum, the town where he was living.

2 Some men from the town came to see Jesus. They brought another man with them who could not move his legs. He was lying on a flat piece of wood. Jesus saw the men. And he knew what they were thinking. They believed that Jesus could cause the man on the bed to be well again. Jesus said to the man who could not move, 'Do not be afraid, my friend. I forgive* you for all the wrong things that you have done.'

3 Then some teachers of the Law* began to speak to each other. 'This man should not have said this', they said to themselves. 'He is speaking as if he is God.'

4 Jesus knew what the teachers were thinking. So he said to them, 'You should not think these bad things. 5 I said to this man, "I forgive* you for all the wrong things that you have done." I could have said to him, "Stand up and walk." 6 But I want you to know this. The Son of Man has authority on earth. He can forgive* people for all the wrong things that they have done.' Then he said to the man who could not move his legs, 'Stand up. Pick up the bed where you are lying. And go home.' 7 So then the man stood up and he went home. 8 The people saw what had happened. They were very surprised and afraid. They saw that God had given much authority to men. So they said, 'God, how great and powerful you are.'

Jesus asks Matthew to come with him

9 Jesus walked away from that place. While he walked, he saw a man called Matthew. He was one of the men who received taxes* for the government. He was sitting in his office. 'Come

with me and be my disciple*', Jesus said. So Matthew stood up and he went with Jesus.

10Later, Jesus went into the house. Many other men who received money for the government came to the house. Jesus was eating a meal there. Many people who had done bad things also came. All these people came to eat a meal with Jesus and his disciples*.

11Some Pharisees* saw all these people eating a meal with Jesus. They asked Jesus' disciples*, 'Why does your teacher eat a meal with these people? They are people who have done bad things. And some of them take tax* money.'

12Jesus heard what the Pharisees* were saying. 'People who are well do not need a doctor', he said to them. 'People who are ill need a doctor. 13Go. And learn what the prophets* wrote down in God's book. God says, "I want people to be kind to each other. I do not only want them to give me gifts in my house." Some people think that they have not done anything wrong. I do not ask such people to be my disciples*. Many people know that they have done wrong things. It is these people that I am asking be my disciples*.'

14Then some of the disciples* of John the Baptist* came to meet Jesus. They asked him, 'We, and the disciples* of the Pharisees*, often stop eating so that we can pray. Why do your disciples* never do that?'

15Jesus answered them with a picture story. 'When the friends of a bridegroom* are with him at his marriage, they do not stop eating. The time will come when people will take the bridegroom* away from his friends. Then his friends will stop eating.'

16 Then Jesus said, 'Nobody uses a piece of new cloth to repair an old coat. If he did, the hole would grow bigger. When someone washed the coat, the new piece of cloth would become smaller. The new cloth would tear the old cloth again and it would make a bigger hole than before.

17Nobody pours new wine* into an old wineskin*. If he
does, then the new wine* will tear the old wineskin*. The
wine* will run out and he will lose it. And he will destroy the
wineskin*. Instead of this, you must put new wine* into a new
wineskin*. Then there will be nothing to destroy the wine* or
the wineskin*.'

Jesus causes a dead girl to become alive again

18While Jesus was saying these things to the people, an
important Jew* came to him. The man went down on his knees
in front of Jesus and said to him, 'My daughter has just died.
Come to my house. Touch her with your hand and then she
will be well again.' 19So Jesus started to go along with the man.
And his disciples* also went along with them.

20A woman was in the crowd near to Jesus. She had lost blood
every day for 12 years. She came close behind Jesus and she
touched the edge of his coat. 21The woman thought, 'If I only
touch his coat, Jesus will cause me to become well again.'

22Jesus turned round and he saw the woman. 'Young woman,
do not be afraid', he said. 'You are well again because
you believed in me.' And immediately the woman became
well again.

23Then Jesus walked on until he arrived at the house of the
important Jew*. He went into the man's house. People there
were making music with pipes made out of wood. The crowd in
the house was also making a loud noise.

24Jesus spoke to everybody in the house. 'Get out of here', he
said. 'This girl is not dead. She is only sleeping.' The people
laughed* at Jesus. 25But the family sent the crowd out of the
house. Then Jesus went into the room where the girl was
lying. He held her hand, and she stood up. 26After that, people
began to tell about what had happened. They told other
people in all that part of the country.

Jesus causes two men to see again

27 Jesus left the house. While he walked along, two men began to follow him. They could not see. They were shouting out to him, 'Son of David, be kind to us and help us.'

28 Jesus went into a house. And the men who could not see came to him. Jesus asked them, 'Do you believe that I can cause your eyes to become well?'

The men replied, 'Yes, Master, we believe that you can do this.'

29 So Jesus touched the men's eyes and he said, 'Because you believed in me, your eyes will become well again.' 30 Then immediately the men could see again. Jesus said to them, 'You must not tell anybody about this.' 31 So the men went away. But then they told everybody in that part of the country all about what Jesus had done for them.

Jesus causes a man to speak again

32 While those two men were leaving Jesus, some people brought another man to him. This man could not talk because a bad spirit* was living inside him. 33 Jesus said to the bad spirit*, 'Leave this man.' The spirit* left him, and the man began to speak. Everybody there was very surprised. They said, 'Nobody has seen anything like this happen in Israel* before.'

34 The Pharisees* said, 'Because Satan* makes him powerful, this man can send bad spirits* out of people.' 35 Jesus went to visit many towns and villages in that part of the country. He taught the people in the places where they met to talk to God. He taught the good news about the Kingdom*. He also caused sick people to become well again from all their illnesses.

Jesus wants God to send out more disciples*

36 When Jesus saw the crowds, he felt sorry for them. The people were anxious*. They had nobody to help them. Jesus

thought, "These people are like sheep with nobody to take care* of them." 37Then Jesus said to his disciples*, 'These people are like many good plants in the fields. The plants are ready for the workers to cut down. But there are not many workers. 38You should ask the master of these fields to send out more workers. Then they can bring in all the plants.'

10

Jesus chooses 12 men to be his apostles*

1 One day, Jesus asked 12 of his disciples* to come to him. He gave them authority over bad spirits* that were living in people. These disciples* could then cause the spirits* to leave people. Jesus also gave them authority to cause sick people to become well again. They could remove all their illnesses.

2These are the names of the 12 apostles*:

The first apostle* is Simon, who is also called Peter.
Then next is Simon's brother called Andrew.
There were James and his brother John, who were Zebedee's sons.
3There were Philip and Bartholomew.
There were Thomas and Matthew. (Matthew received tax* money before he became a disciple*.)
And there was James who was the son of Alphaeus, and Thaddaeus.
4Simon, who was called the Zealot, and Judas Iscariot. Judas Iscariot helped the leaders of the Jews* to take hold of Jesus.

Jesus sends out his 12 apostles*

5Jesus sent out these 12 men. Before they left, he said to them, 'Go only to places where Jews* live. Do not go to any place where the people are not Jews*. And you must not go to any towns where only Samaritans* live.'

⁶'Instead, you must go to the people of Israel*', he said.
'They are like lost sheep with nobody to take care* of them.
⁷While you travel, you must tell people about the Kingdom* of
Heaven*. You must tell them that it has become near. ⁸Make
sick people well again. Cause dead people to become alive
again. And cause people with an illness of the skin to become
well again. Say to bad spirits* that are living in a person,
"Come out of him." Then they will leave the person. I gave
you the authority to do all these things. Now, go and do all
these things for other people. This authority did not cost you
anything. So do not ask them to pay you any money for what
you do. ⁹Do not take any money of any kind in your purse. ¹⁰Do
not take a bag with you, or an extra set of clothes. Do not take
shoes or a stick. People should give a worker everything that
he needs.'

¹¹'When you are travelling, go into towns and villages. Look
for a good person who will take care* of you. You should live in
his house until you leave that town. ¹²When you go into that
man's house, say to the people inside, "I pray that you will be
well." ¹³If the master of the house accepts you, then everyone
in the house will be well. But there may not be anybody in the
house that accepts you. Then ask God not to cause them to
be well. ¹⁴Sometimes you will go into a home or a town and
the people will not accept you. And they will not listen to your
message. Then you should leave that home or that town. And
say to the people, "There is dirt from your town on our feet.
We will clean it off before we leave." ¹⁵I am speaking what is
true', Jesus said to his disciples*. 'One day God will punish* the
people who refuse me. God will punish* them more than he will
punish* the people from Sodom and Gomorrah.'

¹⁶'Listen well. I am sending you to people who will want to
kill you. Your journey will be dangerous. You will be like sheep
among wild dogs. You must watch carefully, like a snake
watches. But you must also be good and kind like a quiet bird.

¹⁷Watch carefully! People will take hold of you and they will
cause you to stand in front of the important Jews*. They will

take you into the places where they meet to talk to God. Then they will hit you with a whip*. ¹⁸People will cause you to stand in front of kings and rulers. This will happen because of me. This is the moment to tell them and those who are not Jews* about me. Tell them the Good News about me. ¹⁹When the people cause you stand in front of kings and rulers, do not be afraid. Do not think about what you should say. Do not be afraid about how you will say things. At that moment, God will tell you the right words to speak. ²⁰You will say words that do not come from you. God the Holy Spirit* will tell you what to say.

²¹Men will cause their own brothers to stand in front of kings and rulers. And these men will say, "Kill him because he believes in Jesus." Fathers will do the same to their own children. Some children will be against their parents. The children will cause their parents to stand in front of kings and rulers and they will say, "Kill my parents because they believe in Jesus." ²²Many people will not like you because you believe in me. But you should never stop believing in me. Then God will save you. ²³If people in one town hurt you because of me, you should leave that town immediately. You should go to another town. What I say is true. You will not have enough time to speak your message in all the towns of Israel*. No, not before the Son of Man comes again.

²⁴A disciple* is not more important than his teacher is. A servant is not more important than his master is. ²⁵A disciple* should be happy if he knows as much as his teacher. A servant should be happy if he is as important as me, his master. Some people call the master of the house Beelzebub (that is "Satan*"). These people will call the people in his house even worse names.

²⁶Do not be afraid of these people. God will remove the cover from everything that people have covered. He will tell everybody all the secrets. ²⁷I tell you secret things. But you must tell these things to the whole world. They must not be secret any longer. I have said things to you that other people

did not hear. But now you must shout all these things from the tops of the houses.'

28 'Do not be afraid of those people who can only kill your body. These people cannot kill your soul*. I say to you that you should be afraid of God. He can kill your body, and then he can also kill your soul* in hell*. 29 Think about this. People sell two small birds for a small coin of little value. One small bird may fall to the ground. But this can only happen if God lets it happen. 30 God even knows how many hairs there are on your head. 31 So do not be afraid of people. God thinks that you are more valuable than many small birds.

32 If a person says to everybody, "I believe in Jesus", then I will speak to God, my Father in heaven*. I will say, "I know that person; he is one of my disciples*." 33 If someone else says to everybody, "I do not believe in Jesus", I will then speak to God, my Father in heaven*. I will say, "I do not know that person; he is not one of my disciples*."

34 I will tell you why I have come into the world. I did not come so that everyone would agree with each other. I came to cause people to be in separate groups that fight against each other.

35 A man will fight against his father.
   A daughter will fight against her mother.
   A woman will fight against her husband's mother.
36 A man's family will fight against him.'

37 'A man must love his own father and mother less than he loves me', said Jesus. 'Then he can be my disciple*. He must also love his own son or daughter less than he loves me. If he does not do this, then he cannot be my disciple*.' 38 Jesus then spoke to the crowd and to his disciples*. 'Perhaps some of you want to be my disciples*', he said. 'If you do, then you cannot think first about yourself. And you cannot think about what you want to do. You must only do what God wants you to do. You must do this every day. You might even have to die. Then you can be one of my disciples*. 39 If a person wants to keep

himself safe, then he will never have true life. But instead, he may die because he believes in me. And then he will have true life for always.'

Jesus teaches the people about God's gifts

40 'If anyone accepts you in his home, then he also accepts me. Anyone who accepts me in his home also accepts God. 41 A person accepts a prophet* into his home because the visitor is a prophet* of God. God will give him the same gift that he gives to a prophet*. A person accepts into his home a good man who obeys God. He only does this because the good man obeys God. God will give that person the same gift that he gives to the good man. 42 A person gives a drink of cold water to one of my least important disciples*. He only does this because that person is one of my disciples*. But it is also true that God will give that man good gifts.'

11

Jesus talks about John the Baptist*

1 When Jesus had finished telling all these things to his disciples*, he went away from that place. And he went to teach people in their towns.

2 At that time, John the Baptist* was in prison. But people told him about all the things that Jesus Christ was doing. So John sent some of his own disciples* to ask Jesus some questions.

3 Then some of the disciples* of John came to Jesus. They said to him, 'John the Baptist* has sent us to you. He wants us to ask you a question. Are you the special person that God has sent to us? If you are not that person, should we wait for someone else?'

4 Jesus replied, 'Go back to John. Tell him what you have seen. Also, tell him what you have heard. 5 People who could not see can see again. People who could not walk can now walk again. Some people who were ill with an illness of the skin are now

well again. Some people who could not hear can now hear again. Some people who were dead now live again. Poor people are hearing the good news. 6 If people are sure about me, they will be happy.'

7 John's disciples* went away again. Then Jesus spoke to the crowd about John. 'You went out to the desert*. You certainly did not go to see the wind blowing against a tall piece of grass. No, you did not go to see that. 8 You certainly did not go to see a man who was wearing expensive soft clothes. No, people like that have many beautiful things and they live in the houses of kings. 9 You went to see a man who receives messages from God's Holy Spirit*. And John was even more important than that. 10 A long time ago, God said this about him:

"I will send someone before you.
He will tell you my message.
He will prepare the road in front of you." '

11 Jesus said, 'John is a very important man. He is greater than any man who has ever lived. But a person who is not great in the Kingdom* of Heaven*, is more important than John.'

12 'From the time that John the Baptist* began to teach until now', Jesus said, 'the Kingdom* of Heaven* is becoming very strong. Strong people who really believe God are taking hold of it. 13 All the prophets* and the books of the Law* spoke God's word. They spoke until the time that John the Baptist* came. 14 The prophets* wrote that Elijah would come back again. They were writing about John, if you can believe it. 15 Everyone who can hear must listen. They must listen to what I say.'

16 Jesus said, 'I will talk to you about the people who are alive today. They are like children who are sitting in the market place. They shout to each other,

17 "We played happy music on a pipe for you, but you did not dance.
We sang a sad song but you did not cry." '

18 'John the Baptist* often stopped eating for some time. He never drank wine*. So you said that a bad spirit* was living inside him. 19 And I, the Son of Man, both eat and drink. So you say about me, "He eats too much and he drinks too much. He is a friend of men who receive taxes* and other bad people." God is good and he understands everything. People who understand my words know this. And they agree with God.'

20 Jesus had done many powerful things for the people to see. But some people in the cities did not believe in him. These people did not want to stop doing wrong things. And they did not want to start obeying God. 21 So Jesus said to them, 'Things will be bad for you, people in Chorazin. And things will be bad for you, people in Bethsaida. I have done great and powerful things in your cities. I did not do them a long time ago in the towns called Tyre and Sidon. If I had done them, the people there would have listened to me. They would then have put on clothes made out of goat's hair. They would also have put ash on their heads. This would have shown God that they were sorry. They would have stopped doing wrong things. And they would have started to obey God. 22 Yes, when God judges* everyone, he will punish* the people from Tyre and Sidon. But he will punish* much more the people from Chorazin and Bethsaida. 23 I will tell you what will happen to the people in Capernaum. They try to lift themselves up to heaven*. He will throw them down to hell*. If I had done these powerful things in Sodom, Sodom would still be standing today. 24 What I say is true. God will punish* the people from Sodom. But he will not punish* them as much as he will punish* the people from Chorazin, Bethsaida and Capernaum.'

25 At this moment, Jesus said, 'Father, you rule over everything in the sky and on the earth! You have taught people who do not know many things. And so I thank you. But you have kept these things a secret from some other people. These people think that they know a lot. And they think that they understand everything. 26 Yes, Father, you chose everything to happen in this way.'

²⁷'My Father has given me all things. And only he knows who
I am. Nobody else really knows that I am the Son. Only I know
who my Father is. Nobody else knows him. But I choose to tell
some people about him.

²⁸Come to me all of you who are tired. You are like people who
have worked for a long time. You are like people who have
carried heavy things. Come to me and you will find a place
to rest.

²⁹Do what I teach you to do. Learn from me everything that is
true. I am very kind and I obey God. Then you will have true
life and you will not be anxious*. ³⁰I will only ask you to do
good things. I will not ask you to carry anything that is too
heavy for you. And I will not ask you to do things that are too
difficult.'

12

The Pharisees* watch what Jesus
does on the Sabbath* day

¹On one Sabbath* day, Jesus was walking through some
fields where wheat* was growing. His disciples* were hungry.
So they began to pick some of the seeds of wheat* and to
eat them. ²Some Pharisees* were with them. And they saw
Jesus' disciples* eating the wheat* seeds. 'Look at what your
disciples* are doing', they said to Jesus. 'It is against God's
Law* to do this on the day that we rest.'

³Jesus said to the Pharisees*, 'King David and his friends were
hungry once. Remember what they did then. You have read
about this. ⁴David went into God's Great House. And he ate
the special bread that was there. He also gave some of it to
his friends. But it is against the Law* for anyone except the
priests* to eat this bread.'

⁵'Also, you should know what God's Law* says. The priests*
are not obeying this Law* when they work in God's Great
House on the Sabbath* day. But God's Law* does not tell

them that they are doing something wrong. 6What I say is true. There is someone here more important than God's Great House. 7A long time ago, a prophet* wrote, "God wants people to be kind to each other. He does not only want you to give him gifts". You do not understand what this really means. If you had understood this, then you would not have said to me, "Your disciples* are doing something wrong." 8The Son of Man has authority over the laws* about the Sabbath* day.'

9Jesus left that place in the fields. He went into the place where the Jews* met to pray. 10A man was in there who had a small hand. It was very weak, so he could not use it. The Pharisees* wanted to say to Jesus that he was doing wrong things. So they asked him, 'Is it right to make someone well again on the Sabbath*?'

11Jesus replied to them, 'One of you may have a sheep that falls into a deep hole on the Sabbath* day. You will take hold of it and you will lift it out of the deep hole. 12Now, a man is much more valuable than a sheep. So our Law* says that we can do good things on the Sabbath* day.'

13Then Jesus said to the man with the weak hand, 'Hold out your hand.' So the man held out his hand. It was now the right size and it was strong. It was the same as his other hand. 14Then the Pharisees* went away from that building where they met. They began to talk to each other about how to kill Jesus.

God chose Jesus to do an important job

15Jesus knew that the Pharisees* wanted to kill him. So he went away from that place. Many people followed him and he caused all the sick people to become well again. 16He said to all these people, 'You must not tell anyone about me.' 17So what the prophet* Isaiah said became true.

18 'Here is my servant.
   I have chosen him to work for me.

I love him and he makes me very happy.
I will give him my Spirit so that he will be powerful.
He will tell people everywhere that I will judge* them.
19 He will not argue or shout at people.
People will not hear him shouting in the streets.
20 He will not hurt weak people.
He will be kind to people who are not strong.
He will do this until there is justice* everywhere.
21 And all people, everywhere, will believe that he can
save them.'

Jesus talks about Satan*

22 After that, some people brought a man to Jesus. The man
could not see and he could not speak because of a bad spirit*
in him. Jesus caused the man to become well again. So then
the man could see and speak again. 23 All the people were very
surprised about what Jesus did. They asked each other, 'Can
Jesus really be the person that God sent to save us?'

24 The Pharisees* also heard about what had happened. 'This
man can cause bad spirits* to come out of people', they said.
'Beelzebub is the ruler of all the bad spirits*. So he is helping
Jesus to do this.'

25 Jesus knew what the Pharisees* were thinking. So he said
to them, 'Maybe groups of people start fighting other groups
of people in the same country. If they do this, then they will
destroy their own country. Or perhaps the people in one city
or one family start fighting each other. Then they will destroy
their own city or family. 26 So, Satan* would not fight against
himself. If Satan* fights against himself, he will soon destroy
his own kingdom*. 27 Some of you Jews* can also send bad
spirits* out of people. Certainly you do not say that Beelzebub
(Satan*) helps them. So your own people show you that you
are wrong about this. 28 I do send bad spirits* out of people.
I use the authority of the Spirit of God to do this. If I do this,
then God is ruling among you. And certainly you must know
that he is.

29Nobody can go into the house of a strong man easily to rob him. To do this, he must first tie up the strong man. Then he can take away all that man's valuable things.' Beelzebub is another name for Satan* or the Devil*. Satan* is like a strong person. But Jesus is like a stronger person. He fights Satan* and beats him. Jesus sends bad spirits* out of people. And they go away. This shows that he is stronger than Satan*. So it was not possible that Satan* was working with Jesus.

30Jesus then said, 'If someone is not working with me, then he is really working against me. If he is not helping me to bring the sheep together, he is against me. He is causing the sheep to run away in different directions. 31God will forgive* all the wrong things that people do against other people. Some people even say bad things against God. And he will forgive* them. Some people say bad things against the Holy Spirit*. But God will never forgive* them for that. 32God will forgive* people who say bad things about me, the Son of Man. But God will not forgive*, now or ever, people who say bad things against the Holy Spirit*.' The Pharisees* had said that Satan* worked with Jesus. It was dangerous to say that. The Holy Spirit* gave his authority and power to Jesus. It was wrong to think that Satan* was helping Jesus.

Jesus talks about a tree and its fruit

33Then Jesus said, 'To have good fruit you must have a good tree. If you have a bad tree, then you will get bad fruit from it. You can know all about every tree by the fruit that it makes. 34You are like the children of dangerous snakes. You cannot say good things when your thoughts are bad. When you speak, your words show what is in your mind. 35The good man says good things because he keeps good thoughts in his mind. The bad man says bad things because he keeps bad thoughts in his mind. 36What I say is true. One day, God will judge* everybody. On that day, you must tell God why you spoke each careless word.

37God will then say to you, "The words that you spoke are good. I will not punish* you." Or God may say to you, "The words that you spoke are bad. So I must punish* you." '

The Pharisees* want to see Jesus do something powerful

38 Then some teachers of the Law* and some Pharisees* spoke to Jesus, 'Teacher, we want to see you do something powerful. This will show us that God sent you.'

39 Jesus replied, 'The people who are alive today are very bad. They do not obey God, but they want him to show them something powerful. But he will not do this. They will see only the same powerful thing that God did to Jonah. 40 Jonah stayed inside a big fish for three days and three nights. In the same way, the Son of Man will remain in the ground for three days and three nights. 41 On the day that God judges* everyone, the people who lived in Nineveh will be there. They also will speak against you who are alive today. They will say that you are bad people. They stopped doing bad things when Jonah spoke to them. And then they obeyed God. Listen! Now there is someone here who is more important than Jonah.'

42 Jesus then said, 'Many years ago, the queen of a country in the south travelled a long way to see King Solomon. She wanted to hear about everything that Solomon knew. So, when God judges* all people, that queen will stand in front of him. And she will speak against you who are alive today. She will say that you are bad people. She listened to Solomon. But there is someone here today. And that person understands things much better than Solomon did. And you are not listening to that person.'

43 And Jesus said, 'When a bad spirit* leaves a person, it travels through dry places. It is looking for somewhere new to live. But it does not find anywhere. So, it says to itself, "I will return to the person, to the place where I lived before." 44 Then it goes back to that person. It finds that the place is clean. Everything inside the place is good, but the place is

empty. 45So the bad spirit* goes out and it brings back 7 worse spirits*. They all go into the person and they live there. Now the person has more bad spirits* than he had before. The same thing will happen to the bad people who are alive today.'

Jesus' mother and brothers come to see him

46While he was still speaking to the crowds, Jesus' mother and brothers arrived. And they stood outside the house. They sent someone inside with a message. 'Tell Jesus that we want to speak to him', they said. 47A crowd was sitting there with Jesus. Someone told him, 'Your mother and brothers are outside the house. They want to speak to you.'

48Jesus replied, 'I will tell you who my mother and brothers are.' 49Then Jesus pointed to his disciples*. 'Look! Here are my mother and my brothers', he said. 50'My brothers and sisters and mother are those people who obey God, my Father in heaven*', said Jesus.

13

Jesus tells a story about a farmer who planted seeds

1Again Jesus left the house and he went down to the Lake Galilee. He sat down to teach. The crowd that came together was very large. So, he climbed into a boat and he sat down. The boat was in the water, and the people stood on the shore. 2Jesus used stories to teach them many things. 3'Listen to me', said Jesus. 'A farmer went out to plant seed in his field. 4While he was throwing the seeds, some fell on the path. The wild birds came and they ate those seeds. 5Some seeds fell on ground with rocks in it. There was not much soil*. The seeds quickly began to grow, because the soil* was not deep. 6But when the sun rose, it burned the young plants. They soon dried up because the soil* was not deep enough for them. 7Some seeds fell among bushes with sharp branches. These weeds grew up with the young plants. The bushes stopped the seeds from growing into strong plants, so the plants did not make any new seeds. [8]Some seeds fell on good soil* and good strong plants grew from those seeds. Some plants made 100 new seeds. Some plants made 60 new seeds and some plants made 30 new seeds.' [9]After Jesus had finished the story, he told the crowd, 'You have ears. So listen well to what I say!'

Jesus explains to his disciples* why he teaches with stories

[10]Then Jesus' disciples* came to him. 'Why do you speak to the crowd with stories?' they asked.

[11]'God has helped you to understand what the stories about the Kingdom* of Heaven* mean. But God has not helped these people to understand about these things. [12]Listen well. God will help the person who wants to understand my words. He will then really understand a lot more. Another person understands very little. God will take away the little that he has. So then he will understand nothing at all. [13]The reason I use stories to talk to other people is this:

"So these people look. But they do not see.
 So they listen. But they do not hear or understand." '

[14]'Isaiah, the prophet*, wrote a message from God about this. And now that message has become true.

"This people will listen and listen. But they will not understand.
 They will look and look. But they will not see anything.
[15] The people do not really want to understand.
 They are like people who have shut their ears.
 They are like people who have shut their eyes.
 If they did want to look, then they would see.
 If they did want to listen, then they would hear.
 And then they would understand everything and they would turn back.
 And if they did turn back, then I would make them well."

16 You should be happy because God has helped you to see.
And he has helped you to hear. 17 What I say is true. Many
prophets* and good people from a long time ago wanted to
see these things. But they did not see the things that you can
see. They wanted to hear the things that you are hearing. But
they did not hear them.'

Jesus explains the story about the
farmer who planted his seeds

18 'Listen to me now. I will explain to you what this story about
the farmer means. 19 Some seeds fell on the path. The path is
like people who do not understand the message. They hear it
but they do not understand it. Then the devil* comes quickly
to them. And he takes away what they have heard. 20 Some of
the seeds fell on soil* with rocks in it. This soil* is like some
people who hear the message from God. They are happy to
believe it for a while. But it does not go into their lives and
thoughts. 21 They believe in God for a while. But they are like
plants that do not grow down in the soil*. Because they obey
God's words, other people give them problems. So when they
meet trouble or difficulty, they stop believing. 22 Some seeds
fell among weeds. This soil* is like other people who hear the
message from God. But they have many anxieties*. They think
that more money and other valuable things will cause them
to be happy. These thoughts stop them obeying God. They
are like plants that do not grow new seeds. 23 But some seeds
fell on good soil*. This soil* is like other people who hear the
message from God. They understand it and they obey God.
These people are like good plants. From one seed, the good
plants make 30 seeds. Other good plants make 60 new seeds,
and some good plants make 100 new seeds.'

Jesus tells a story about some weeds

24 Then Jesus told the people another story. 'This is what
the Kingdom* of Heaven* is like', he said. 'A farmer planted
some good wheat* seeds into his field. 25 But one night, when

everyone was sleeping, a bad person came to the farmer's field. He did not like the farmer. This bad person planted seeds from weeds among the good seeds. Then the bad person went away again. 26 The good seeds grew and the plants began to make seeds. But when this happened, the weeds also grew.

27 So the farmer's servants came to speak to him. "Master, many weeds are now growing in the ground where you planted the wheat* seeds. How did this happen?" they asked him.

28 The farmer said to his servants, "A bad person who does not like me has done this."

"Do you want us to go and pull up the weeds?" the servants then asked the farmer.

29 "No", replied the farmer. "I do not want you to do that. If you pull up the weeds, you will also pull up some of the wheat* plants. 30 Let the good plants and the weeds grow up together. After that, it will be time for the workers to cut the plants that have large seeds. They will bring them inside from the fields. I will ask the workers to cut the weeds down first. They can tie them together and burn them. Then they can cut the wheat* and bring it into my building. I can store it there." '

Jesus tells a story about a small seed

31 Jesus told the people another story. 'I will tell you again what the Kingdom* of Heaven* is like', he said. 'It is like a very small seed. A man took this seed and he planted it in his field. 32 It is the smallest seed in the world. But when it starts to grow, it becomes bigger than the largest bush. It will become a tree. The wild birds will come and they will make places to live among the branches of that tree.'

Jesus tells a story about yeast*

33 Jesus told the people another story. 'I will tell you another story about what the Kingdom* of Heaven* is like', he said. 'It is like some yeast* and flour. A woman took the yeast* and she

mixed it in three large bowls of flour. The yeast* grew and it caused all the bread to rise.'

34 Jesus told the crowd all these things. But he only used stories to teach them. 35 So what the prophet* had said became true:

> 'I will use stories when I speak to them.
> And I will teach them secret things.
> People have never learned these things before.'

36 Then Jesus went away from the place where the crowd was. He went into the house where he was staying. And his disciples* also came into the house with him. 'Explain to us the story about the weeds in the soil*', they said to Jesus.

Jesus explains the story about the weeds

37 Jesus replied to his disciples*, 'The Son of Man is like the farmer who planted the wheat* seed in the field. 38 The field is like the world. The good wheat* seeds are like the people who belong to the Kingdom*. The weeds are like the people who belong to Satan*. 39 Satan* is the bad person who planted the weed seeds in the field. The moment when the workers cut down all the plants is like the end of time. God's angels* are the workers who cut the plants down.

40 The workers cut the weeds and they burn them in the fire. In the same way, the angels* will do this at the end of time. They will do it to the people who belong to Satan*. 41 The Son of Man will send his angels*. They will take away all the people who are not really part of his Kingdom*. They have caused other people not to obey God. And the angels* will take away all the people who have not obeyed God. 42 The angels* will throw the bad people into the great fire. There the people will cry. And they will bite their teeth together because they are angry. 43 The people who obeyed God will shine like the sun. They will be in the Kingdom* of their Father. You have ears, so listen well to what I say.'

Jesus tells a story about a man who found valuable things in the ground

⁴⁴'I can tell you again what the Kingdom* of Heaven* is like', Jesus said. 'The Kingdom* of Heaven* is like something valuable that a man buried in a field. Another man found it, but then he covered it over again with dirt. Then that second man was very happy and he went away. He sold everything that he had. Then he went and bought the field with the valuable things in it.'

Jesus tells a story about some valuable stones

⁴⁵'I will tell you again what the Kingdom* of Heaven* is like', Jesus said. 'A man has a business. He looks for beautiful valuable stones that he can buy. ⁴⁶One day he found a very beautiful and very valuable stone that someone wanted to sell. So he went away. And he sold everything that he had. Then he went and he bought that very beautiful and very valuable stone.

⁴⁷I can tell you again what the Kingdom* of Heaven* is like', Jesus said. 'Some men had nets* to catch fish in. They threw their nets* into the lake and they caught many different kinds of fish. ⁴⁸When the net* was full of fish, the men pulled it up on to the shore. Then they sat down. Some of the fish were good to eat, and they put these fish into baskets. Some of the fish were not good to eat, and they threw these fish away. ⁴⁹This is what will happen at the end of time. God will send his angels*. They will put the people who did not obey God in one place. And they will put the people who obey God in another place. ⁵⁰The angels* will throw the people who did not obey God into the great fire. There the people will cry. They will also bite their teeth together because they are angry.'

⁵¹Then Jesus asked his disciples*, 'Have you understood all these things?' 'Yes, we have', they replied.

[52] 'Some teachers of the Law* have learned about the Kingdom* of Heaven*', Jesus said. 'These men are like the master of a house. The master takes out some old things and also some new things from the place where he stores them.'

[53] When Jesus had finished telling these stories, he went away from that place.

Jesus goes to Nazareth

[54] Jesus went to the town called Nazareth. He had lived in Nazareth when he was a boy. He taught the people in the building where they met to pray. The people were very surprised about the things that he was teaching them. 'Where did this man learn all these things?' they asked each other. 'How does he know so much? How does he do all these powerful things?' they said. [55] 'We know who this man is. He is the son of a man who makes things out of wood. And Mary is his mother. We also know his brothers, James, Joseph, Simon and Judas. [56] All his sisters also live here in this town among us. So then, where did he learn to do all these things? Who caused him to be so powerful?' So the people were not happy with Jesus.

[57] 'People do not believe a prophet* who comes from their own town', Jesus said to them. 'His own people and his own family do not believe that he receives messages from God. Only people in other places believe him.'

[58] Jesus did not do many powerful things in Nazareth because the people did not believe in him.

14

Herod's soldiers kill John the Baptist*

[1] At that time, Herod the ruler heard reports about the things that Jesus was doing.

2 'That man Jesus is really John the Baptist*', said Herod to his men. 'John was dead but he has become alive again. That is the reason that Jesus can do all these powerful things.'

3 Herod himself had said to his soldiers, 'Take hold of John. Tie his hands and feet and put him in prison.' Herod had done this because of his wife Herodias. Before Herod married her, she was the wife of Herod's brother Philip. 4 Because Herod had married her, John had said to him, 'Herodias was your brother's wife. So you did not do the right thing when you married her.'

5 Herod wanted to tell his soldiers that they must kill John. But the people thought that John was a prophet*. So Herod was afraid to kill him.

6 But when it was Herod's birthday, he had a special meal. The daughter of Herodias danced in front of him and his visitors. Her dance caused Herod to become very happy. 7 'Ask me for anything that you want', Herod said. 'And I will give it to you. God is listening to me say this.' 8 Herodias suggested to her daughter, 'Ask Herod to give you John's head.' So her daughter asked Herod to give her the head of John the Baptist* on a plate. 9 Then Herod was sad, but he had spoken a special promise in front of God. So he could not refuse her. And his visitors had heard him. So he sent his men to give Herodias's daughter what she had asked for. 10 He immediately said to a soldier, 'Cut off John's head and bring it here.' So, the soldier went to the prison and he cut off John's head. 11 Then he brought it back on a plate and he gave it to the girl. She then gave it to her mother. 12 John's disciples* heard the news that John was dead. So, they went to the prison and they took away his body. And then they buried it. After that, they went to see Jesus. And they told him what had happened.

Jesus gives food to 5000 men and their families

13 Jesus heard about what had happened to John. After that, he went away from that place. He sailed in a boat to a quiet

place where he could be alone. But the crowd heard where Jesus had gone. So they left their towns and they followed Jesus. They walked to the place where he was. ¹⁴Jesus climbed out of the boat to the shore. He saw a large crowd there. He loved them and he felt sorry for them. He saw that there were sick people in the crowd. So he made them well again.

¹⁵When it was almost evening, Jesus' disciples* came to speak to him. They said to him, 'We are in a place where there are no houses. And it will soon be dark. So send the crowd away now, so that they can go to the villages near here. There they can buy some food for themselves to eat.'

¹⁶'The people do not need to go away. You give them some food to eat', Jesus replied.

¹⁷'But we only have 5 small loaves of bread and two fish', they said.

¹⁸'Bring the bread and fish here to me', Jesus said. ¹⁹Then Jesus said to the large crowd, 'Sit down on the grass.' Jesus received the 5 loaves of bread and two fish from his disciples*. He looked up to the sky and he thanked God for the bread and the fish. Then he broke the bread into pieces. And he gave it to his disciples* to give to the crowd. ²⁰Then everybody ate, and they all had enough. Then the disciples* picked up all the food that the people had not eaten. And they filled 12 baskets with broken pieces of bread and fish. ²¹About 5000 men ate the bread and fish. The women and children also ate it with them.

Jesus walks on the water

²²Immediately after this, Jesus said to his disciples*, 'Get in the boat and sail across the lake. Go on in front of me while I send the crowd away.' ²³Then he sent the crowd away. After they had gone, he went up on a mountain alone to pray. And he was still there alone when it became dark. ²⁴Now, the boat was in the middle of the lake. The wind was blowing against the boat and the water was hitting it.

25 Then, when it was very early in the morning, Jesus walked across the water towards his disciples*. 26 And the disciples* saw him walking on top of the water. They were very frightened. 'It is a spirit', they said. And they shouted with loud voices because they were afraid.

27 But immediately, Jesus spoke to them. 'Be brave! Do not be afraid! It is I, Jesus', he said to them.

28 Peter replied, 'Sir', he said, 'are you really Jesus? Then say to me, "Come here! Walk on top of the water." '

29 'Come to me', said Jesus.

So Peter climbed out of the boat. He walked on top of the water and he came towards Jesus. 30 But then Peter saw that the wind was still blowing against him. He became afraid and he began to go down into the water. He shouted to Jesus, 'Master, save me!'

31 Immediately, Jesus put out his hand and he took hold of Peter. 'Why do you not really believe in me to help you?' he said to Peter. 'Why did you not believe that I could cause you to walk on the water?'

32 When Jesus and Peter climbed into the boat, the strong wind stopped blowing. 33 The disciples* who were in the boat went down on their knees in front of Jesus. 'It is true. You are the person that God calls his son', they said.

34 When they had sailed across the lake to the shore, they climbed out of the boat. They were in the part of the country called Gennesaret.

35 The people who lived in that part of the country recognised Jesus. So they sent people to tell everyone in that part of the country that Jesus was there. They brought all their sick people to see him. 36 They asked Jesus to let them touch the edge of his clothes. And Jesus caused every sick person who touched his clothes to become well again.

15

Jesus tells the Pharisees* and teachers of the Law* to obey God

¹After that, a group of Pharisees* and teachers of the Law* came from Jerusalem to talk to Jesus. ²These men spoke to Jesus. 'Our ancestors* taught us the right way to do everything. Why do your disciples* not obey the things that our ancestors* taught us? They do not wash their hands in the right way before they eat a meal.'

³'Yes, God tells us the right way to obey him', Jesus replied. 'But you do not obey God. Instead, you do the things that you have taught the people to do. ⁴Moses wrote in his law*, "God says that you must love your father and mother. Do good things for them and only say good things about them." God also said, "Someone should kill a person who says bad things about his own father or mother." ⁵But instead of obeying this, you teach people something different. You let a person say to his father or mother, "I would have given these good gifts to you, but I cannot. Instead, I have given them to God." Then, you let him give nothing to his mother and father. ⁶When you let a person do this, you have not obeyed God's Law*. You have obeyed the laws* of your ancestors* instead. You do many other things like this. ⁷You are hypocrites*! What Isaiah said about you is true. He wrote down these words from God:

⁸ "These people say good things about me,
　but they do not really want to obey me.
⁹ They say that I am powerful and important.
　But what they say has no purpose.
　They teach their own rules, which I did not give to them." '

Jesus talks about the wrong things that people do

¹⁰Jesus asked all the people to come together near him. 'Listen to me', he said, 'so that you can understand my words. ¹¹God

will not say to a person, "I will not accept you because you ate a certain food." It is not the food that a person eats. Food does not cause God to say, "I cannot accept you." Instead, what comes out of his mouth is important. This can cause God to say, "I will not accept you." '

¹²Jesus' disciples* went near to him and they said, 'The Pharisees* heard what you said to them. They are not happy with what you said. Do you know that?'

¹³Jesus replied to his disciples*, 'Those Pharisees* are like plants that God, my Father in heaven*, did not put in the soil*. He will pull all these plants out of the soil*. ¹⁴Do not be anxious* about them. They cannot see, but they are telling people which way to go. A man who cannot see does not show another man like himself where to go. If he does this, then both men will fall into a deep hole in the road.'

¹⁵Peter said to Jesus, 'Explain to us what you just said.'

¹⁶'You still cannot understand what I am saying. You are like the Pharisees* and the teachers of the Law*', replied Jesus. ¹⁷'The food that a person eats first goes into his mouth. Then it goes into his stomach, and then it goes out of his body. ¹⁸The words that a person speaks come from their thoughts. So what a person says can cause God to say to him, "I will not accept you." ¹⁹A person can think bad thoughts. These thoughts may cause him to kill somebody. Or they may cause him to have sex with another man's wife. He might rob somebody. He might say things that are not true about someone. Or he might say bad things about somebody.'

²⁰'All these bad things cause God to say to a person, "I cannot accept you." But perhaps a man does not wash his hands before he eats. This does not cause God to say, "I will not accept you." '

Jesus makes a girl well again

21 After that, Jesus left Gennesaret and he went to some places near to the cities called Tyre and Sidon.

22 A woman was living in this part of the country. She was one of the people from the group called the Canaanites. She went to see Jesus and she continued to shout with a loud voice to him. 'Son of David, help me, sir. A bad spirit* is living inside my daughter. It is making her very ill.'

23 Jesus did not reply to the woman. So his disciples* came to him. 'Please, please send this woman away', they said. 'She is following us and she is making a lot of noise.'

24 Jesus replied to his disciples*, 'God sent me only to the people of Israel*, because they are like lost sheep.'

25 The woman came to Jesus and she went down on her knees in front of him. 'Sir, please help me', she said.

26 Jesus did answer the woman this time. 'It is not right to take bread from the children and then to throw it to the dogs.'

27 The woman replied to Jesus. 'Yes sir, that is true. But even the dogs eat the small pieces of bread that fall from their master's table.'

28 'You are a woman who believes very well in me', said Jesus. 'So God will do what you asked.' And immediately, the woman's daughter became well again.

29 Jesus travelled on from that place and he walked along the shore of Lake Galilee. He climbed up a hill and he sat down there. 30 A large crowd came to him and they brought sick people with them. Some of these sick people could not walk very well, and some of them could not see. Some of the sick people had arms or legs that hurt. And some of them could not speak. There were also many other sick people who had different illnesses. Their friends put the sick people in front of Jesus. And Jesus caused them all to become well again. 31 The

large crowd were very surprised about what they saw. People who could not speak could now speak again. Those people who could not walk very well could now walk well. The people who could not see could now see. They were all saying to God, 'God of Israel*, you are powerful. You are great. You are very important. We thank you because you are so kind.'

Jesus feeds 4000 men and their families

32 Then Jesus spoke to his disciples*, 'Come near to me. I feel sorry for this crowd', he said. 'They have stayed with me now for three days and they have no more food. I do not want to send them away while they are hungry. They may fall down on the way because they are weak and hungry.'

33 The disciples* said to Jesus, 'We are in a place that is a long way from any town. Where can we find enough bread here to feed so many people?'

34 'How many loaves of bread do you have?' asked Jesus.

'We have 7 loaves of bread and a few small fish', they replied.

35 Jesus said to the crowd, 'Sit down on the ground.' 36 Then he held the 7 loaves and the fish in his hands and he thanked God for them. Then he broke the bread and the fish into pieces and he gave the food to his disciples*. 'Give this food to the people', he said. 37 All the people ate and they all had enough. After the people had finished eating, there remained a lot of extra food. Jesus' disciples* filled 7 baskets with the extra pieces of bread and fish. 38 4000 men ate the bread and fish. This number did not include the women and children who also ate. 39 Then Jesus spoke to the large crowd again. 'Now you should all go home', he said. After that, Jesus got into the boat. And they sailed away to the part of the country called Magadan.

16

The Pharisees* ask again to see something powerful

¹Some Pharisees* and Sadducees* went to see Jesus. They
wanted to make Jesus do something wrong. 'Do something
powerful for us to see', they asked him. 'Then we will know
that God sent you.'

²Jesus answered them. 'Sometimes the sky is red in the
evening. Then you say that tomorrow the weather will be good.
³Sometimes the sky is red in the morning and the sky has dark
clouds in it. Then you say that today there will be a storm.
You can look at the sky. And then you know what weather is
coming. But special things are happening now. And you do not
understand what they mean. ⁴The people who are alive today
are very bad. They do not obey God. They want God to show
them something powerful. No! God will not show you anything.
You will only see the same powerful thing that God did to
Jonah.' So Jesus went away and left them.

Jesus talks about the yeast* of the
Pharisees* and the Sadducees*

⁵Then Jesus and his disciples* went over to the other side of
the lake. His disciples* forgot to take any bread with them.
⁶'Be careful', Jesus said to them. 'You must be careful and
watch for the yeast* of the Pharisees* and Sadducees*.'

⁷The disciples* began to talk to each other about this. 'Jesus
is saying this because we did not bring any bread with us',
they said.

⁸Jesus knew what they were talking about. So he said to them,
'You should not be talking about the fact that you did not
bring any bread with you. You still do not believe very much in
me. ⁹You still do not understand. You should remember when
I used 5 loaves of bread to give food to 5000 men and their
families. You should remember how many baskets of bread

you filled after the meal. 10 You should remember when I used
7 loaves of bread to give food to 4000 men and their families.
You should remember how many baskets of bread you filled
after the meal. 11 I spoke about the yeast* of the Pharisees*
and the Sadducees*. I said that you must be careful about
it. You should have understood that this time I was not really
speaking about bread.' 12 Then the disciples* understood what
Jesus was talking about. They did not need to be careful about
the yeast* that they used in their bread. They must be careful
about what the Pharisees* and Sadducees* taught.

Peter says who Jesus is

13 Jesus went into the part of the country called Caesarea
Philippi. While he was there, he asked his disciples* a question.
'Tell me', he said. 'When people talk about the Son of Man,
what do they say?'

14 'Some people say that you are John the Baptist*', they
replied. 'Other people say that you are Elijah. And some other
people say that you are Jeremiah, or another prophet*.'

15 'What do you think', he asked them. 'Who am I?'

16 Simon Peter answered him. 'You are the Christ*. God sent
you. You are the Son of the God who is alive.'

17 Jesus said to Simon Peter, 'Simon, son of Jonah, God has
given help to you. No person on earth taught you that. God,
my Father, who rules in heaven*, taught you this. 18 What I say
is true. You are called Peter, which means a rock. And I will
build my Church on this rock. Not even the power of death can
beat and destroy my Church. 19 I will give you the keys to the
Kingdom* where God rules in heaven*. Perhaps you will say,
"No, you cannot do that" to something that people want on
earth. Then God will say "No" to it where he rules in heaven*.
Maybe you will say, "Yes, you can do that" to something that
people want on earth. Then God will say "Yes" to it where he
rules in heaven*.'

20 Jesus spoke with authority to his disciples*. 'Do not tell anyone that I am the Christ*.'

Jesus tells his disciples* how he would die

21 After this, Jesus began to explain everything to his disciples*. 'I must go to Jerusalem', he told them. 'There, people will cause me to have great pain. The leaders of the Jews*, the important priests*, and the teachers of the Law* will hurt me. And then people will kill me. But three days later, God will cause me to be alive again.'

22 Then Peter led Jesus away from the other disciples*. Peter did not agree with what Jesus had said. He spoke with strong words to Jesus. 'No, Sir', he said. 'You must not say these things. I pray that God will never let this happen!'

23 Jesus turned towards Peter and said to him, 'Go away from me, Satan*. I must obey God. But you are trying to stop me. Your thoughts do not come from God. Instead, you are thinking as men think.'

24 Then Jesus said to his disciples*, 'Someone may want to come with me', he said. 'Then he must leave what he himself wants to do. He must carry a cross* and he must be ready to die with me. 25 If a person wants to keep his life safe, he will lose it. But instead, he may die because he believes in me. And then he will have true life, which has no end. 26 A person could get the whole world for himself. This would not be good for him if he died as a result. There is nothing that a person can give to get back his life. 27 I tell you all this because I, the Son of Man, will come back here with God's angels*. When I come, I will be powerful and important like God my Father. I will pay each person for what he has done on earth. 28 What I am saying now is true. I will tell you something about the people who are standing here. Some of them will not die until they see the Son of Man's kingdom begin.'

17

God causes Jesus to become different to look at

¹ Six days later, Jesus took Peter and the brothers James and John with him. He led them up a high mountain where they were alone together. ² Peter, James and John watched Jesus and they saw him become different to look at. His face was bright and it shone like the sun. His clothes became very white and they shone. ³ Then Peter, James and John saw two men appear in front of them. These two men were Moses and Elijah and they were talking with Jesus.

⁴ Peter said to Jesus, 'Teacher, it is a good thing that we are here. Let us build three huts. One hut will be for you. One hut will be for Moses and one hut will be for Elijah.'

⁵ While Peter was still speaking, a bright cloud appeared. And it covered them all. They heard a voice, which came out from the cloud. 'This is my Son', it said. 'I love him and he makes me very happy. Listen to him.'

⁶ When the disciples* heard the person speaking, they threw themselves down. And their faces touched the ground. They were very frightened. ⁷ But Jesus came to them and he touched them. 'Stand up again', he said. 'Do not be afraid.' ⁸ When they looked up, they could not see anyone else. Only Jesus was there.

⁹ While they were walking down the mountain again, Jesus spoke to Peter, James and John. 'You must not tell anyone about what you have just seen', he said. 'One day, the Son of Man will die and then become alive again. Then you can tell people about these things.'

¹⁰ Then the three disciples* asked Jesus a question. 'The teachers of the Law* say, "Elijah will return to earth first before anything else happens." Why do they say this?'

11 'Yes, Elijah does come first', said Jesus. 'He causes everything to be ready. 12 But I tell you that Elijah has already come. People did not recognise him. They did all the bad things to him that they wanted to do. In the same way, they will also hurt me, the Son of Man.' 13 Then the disciples* understood that he was really talking about John the Baptist*.

Jesus makes a boy well

14 Then Jesus, Peter, James and John returned to the place where the crowd was waiting for them. A man came to see Jesus. He went down on his knees in front of him. 15 'Teacher', he said. 'please be kind to my son. His mind is sick. Sometimes he does not know what he is doing. Often he falls into the fire, or he falls into water. 16 I brought the boy to your disciples*. But they could not make him well.'

17 'You people today still do not believe in me', Jesus said. 'You have turned away from God. I have lived here among you for a long time. I cannot remain with you much longer. Now it is difficult for me to be patient with you.' Jesus then said to the man, 'Bring your son here to me.' 18 Jesus said to the bad spirit*, 'Stop!' Then the bad spirit* left the boy and immediately he became well.

19 When the disciples* were alone with Jesus, they asked him, 'Why could we not cause the bad spirit* to leave the boy?'

20 'You could not do it because you do not believe well in me', Jesus replied. 'What I say is true. If you believe in God even a little bit, then you can do great things. You can say to this mountain, "Move from this place to that other place." And it will move. You can do anything. 21 But you must pray and not eat for a time. That will cause this kind of spirit* to leave a person', said Jesus.

22 When Jesus and his disciples* all met together in Galilee, he said, 'Soon people will put the Son of Man into the hands of powerful men. 23 These men will kill him. But he will be alive again three days later.' The disciples* were very sad.

24After that, Jesus and his disciples* arrived at Capernaum. Some men who received taxes* went to talk to Peter. They asked him, 'Does your teacher pay the tax* for God's Great House?'

25'Yes', said Peter to them. 'My teacher does pay the tax*.'

Then Peter returned to the house where Jesus was staying. He wanted to tell Jesus what had just happened. But Jesus spoke first. 'Here is a question for you to answer, Simon', he said. 'Who are the people who must pay taxes* and money to the rulers of the world? Do the rulers take taxes* from their own sons? Or do they take taxes* from other people?'

26'The kings take the taxes* from other people', Simon replied.

Jesus said to him, 'This means that people from the ruler's own country do not need to pay anything. 27But we do not want to make these men who take the tax* angry. So go to the lake and throw out a line to fish with. And pull up the first fish that you catch on your line. Open the mouth of the fish and you will find a gold coin inside it. Take the coin and give it to those who receive tax*. This will be enough money for both my tax* and yours.'

18

Jesus says who is the most important person

1Soon after this, the disciples* came to Jesus and they asked him, 'Who is the most important person in the Kingdom* of Heaven*?'

2There was a little child there. Jesus said to the child, 'Come here. Stand in front of everybody.' 3'What I say is true', Jesus said. 'Unless you become like a child, you cannot come into the Kingdom* of Heaven*. 4This little child does not think that he is very important. You must also think as he does. A person who does this will be the most important person in the Kingdom* of Heaven*.

5 Any person who accepts a child because of me also
accepts me.'

Jesus talks about causing people to do wrong things

6 'Maybe someone will cause a little person to stop believing
in me', said Jesus. 'It would be better for this person if other
people hung a big stone round his neck. Then they could throw
that bad person into the deep sea together with the stone.

7 It is very bad that some things in the world cause people
to do wrong things. You can be sure that bad things will
come. But God will punish* the person who makes these bad
things happen.'

8 'Maybe your hand or your foot causes you to do wrong things.
Then you should cut it off. And you should throw it away. It is
better to have only one hand or one foot and to have God's
true life. It is much worse to keep both hands and both feet
and do wrong things. Then God will throw you into hell*. 9 If
your eye causes you to do wrong things, then you should take
it out. You should throw it away. It is better to have only one
of your eyes and have God's true life. It is much worse if God
throws you with your two eyes into hell*. There the fire does
not ever stop burning.

10 Be careful that you do not think that these little people are
not important. What I say is true. The angels* who watch over
them always remain with my Father in his home. And those
angels* speak to him.'

[11 The Son of Man has come to save that which was lost.]

12 'Think about a man who has 100 sheep. He counts them. And
he discovers that one of his sheep is not there. So he leaves all
the other sheep on the hills. Then he goes to look for the lost
sheep. 13 What I say is true. The man will be very happy if he
finds that lost sheep. All the other sheep are safe on the hill.
But they do not make him as happy as this sheep does. They
were never lost. 14 God, who is my Father in heaven*, is like

this man. He does not want even one of these little people to be lost.'

A friend does wrong things against you

15 'If your brother has done wrong things against you, then you must go to him. You can talk about it together when you are alone with him. Then he may understand that you are right. If he does understand, then you can call him your friend again.'

16 'Maybe he does not want to listen to you. Then take one or two other people with you to him. These one or two people then know what wrong things your brother has done. They will know what you said to him. They will know that it is true. God's word said that we should do this. 17 If your brother will not listen to the two or three of you, go to the Church. Tell other people what has happened. Let those who obey me speak to your brother. If he is not sorry, stop being his friend. He is like somebody who refuses to obey God.'

18 'What I say is true. Maybe you will say, "No, you cannot do that" to something that people on earth want to do. God will say "No" to it where he rules in heaven*. Maybe you will say, "Yes, you can do that" to something that people want on earth. God will then say "Yes" to it where he rules in heaven*.

19 Two people may agree together to ask God for the same thing. Then my Father above will give them what they ask for.

20 Two or more people come together to speak to me because they believe in me. I am there with them.'

Jesus tells the people about the
servant who did not forgive*

21 Then Peter came to talk to Jesus. 'Teacher', he asked. 'If my brother does wrong things against me many times, how many times must I forgive* him? Must I forgive* him as many as 7 times for the wrong things that he has done against me?'

22 'I do not say 7 times', Jesus replied. 'I say, 7 times, and then again and again until you cannot count.'

23 'I will tell you what the Kingdom* of Heaven* is like. A king wanted to check how much money his servants should give to him. 24 So the king began to check. Then his men led a servant to him who had a big debt. He must pay back 10 000 gold coins to the king.'

25 'The servant could not pay his debt to the king. So the king said to his men, "Sell the servant and his wife and children and all his things. Then I will keep the money to pay his debt."

26 Then the servant went down on his knees in front of the king. He said to him, "Please, please give me some more time, then I will pay you everything." 27 Then the king felt sorry for his servant and said to him, "You do not need to give me the money. You are free of the debt."

28 But then that same servant went away and he met another servant of the king. This other servant had to pay back a debt of 100 cheap coins to the first servant. The first servant took hold of the neck of the other servant. "Give me the money that is mine", he said.

29 The other servant went down on his knees in front of the first servant. "Please, please give me some more time", he said to the first servant. "Then I will give you the money."

30 But the first servant said, "I refuse to do that!" And he put the other servant in prison until he could pay his debt to him. 31 The other servants of the king saw what had happened. They were not happy about it. So they went to see the king. And they told him about everything that had happened.

32 So the king then sent a message to bring the first servant to him. "You are a very bad person", said the king to the servant. "I told you that you did not need to give me my money. I did this because you asked me. 33 You should be kind to the other servant in the same way that I was kind to you." 34 The king was very angry with the first servant. His men put the first

servant in prison and they punished* him. He would remain there until he could pay all his debt to the king.'

35 Then Jesus finished the story and he said, 'You must forgive* your friend completely. If you do not forgive* him completely, then, in the same way, my Father above will not forgive* you.'

19

Jesus teaches about when a man sends his own wife away

1 When Jesus had finished saying all these things, he went away from Galilee. He went to the part of Judea that is on the other side of the river Jordan. 2 Large crowds followed Jesus there. Jesus caused the sick people in the crowds to become well again.

3 Some Pharisees* came to talk to Jesus. They tried to cause Jesus to give the wrong answers to their questions. They asked, 'Can a man send his own wife away and say to her, "You are no longer my wife." Does the Jewish* Law* let him do this for any reason he chooses?'

4 'You surely have read about this in God's book', Jesus replied. 'At the start of the world, God made men and he also made women.'

5 'Because of this, a man leaves his father and his mother. God joins him and his wife together. The man and the woman become like one person. 6 They are not two separate people any longer. They are like one person. God has joined them together to be husband and wife. So nobody must separate them.'

7 Then the Pharisees* said to Jesus, 'Moses said that a man could give his own wife a paper. The paper shows that the man and woman are now separate. Then the man can send the woman away. Why did Moses say this?'

8 Jesus answered them. 'Moses said this because you people did not want to obey God. All these things were different at the start, when he made the world. 9 What I say is true. A man must not send his wife away unless she has had sex with another man. A man can only marry another woman if that has happened. If not, then he does a wrong thing if he marries another woman.'

10 Jesus' disciples* replied, 'This is what it is like for a man and a woman to marry. Maybe it is better if a man does not marry.'

11 Jesus then answered, 'Not everyone can agree with this idea. God has not given it to everyone. 12 What I say is true. There are several different reasons why a man cannot marry. Some men cannot have sex. They were born like that. Some other men also cannot have sex. This is because men did something to them. And now they cannot have sex. Some men do not marry because they can work better for God without a wife. Anyone who can understand this can agree with it.'

Jesus wants children to come to him

13 Then some people brought their children to Jesus. They wanted him to put his hands on their children's heads. They wanted him to pray for their children. But the disciples* did not like this. They said to them, 'Take your children away from here.'

14 But Jesus said, 'Do not stop the children. Let them come to me. People who are like these children can come into the Kingdom* of Heaven*.' 15 So Jesus put his hands on each of the children's heads and he prayed for them. Then, after that, he went away from that place.

Jesus meets a rich man

16 One day a man came to see Jesus. 'Teacher', he asked. 'What good thing must I do so that I can live for always?'

¹⁷Jesus replied, 'You should not ask me about a good thing! Only God is good. If you want to live for always, then you must obey all God's laws*.'

¹⁸The man asked Jesus, 'Which laws* must I obey? '

So Jesus replied, 'Do not kill anyone. Do not have sex with anyone who is not your wife. Do not rob anyone. Always say true things about people. ¹⁹Love your father and your mother and only say good things about them. Love other people as much as you love yourself.'

²⁰'I have always obeyed these laws*', the young man replied. 'What else must I do?'

²¹'If you want to be completely good', Jesus said to him, 'then you must do this. You must sell everything that you have. Give the money to poor people and then you will have valuable things in heaven*. Come back when you have done that. And then follow me.'

²²When the young man heard this, he was not happy. Then he went away. He was feeling sad because he was a very rich man.

²³Then Jesus said to his disciples*, 'What I say is true. It is very difficult for a rich man to come into the Kingdom* of Heaven*. ²⁴Yes, it is difficult for a big animal to go through the hole in a needle*. But it is much more difficult than that for a rich man to come into the Kingdom* of Heaven*.'

²⁵When the disciples* heard this, they were even more surprised. 'Who then can God save?' they asked.

²⁶Jesus looked at them and he replied, 'Men cannot save themselves. But God can do it. God can do everything.'

²⁷'Listen!' Peter said to Jesus. 'We have left everything that we had. And now we are your disciples*. What will we receive because we have done this?'

²⁸Jesus said to his disciples*, 'What I say is true. The Son of Man will rule in the new world that will start one day. You who

are my disciples* will also rule. You will judge* the 12 families
of Israel*. 29Some people may leave their house or brothers
or sisters or mother or father or children or fields. They leave
them to go and tell other people the good news about me.
Those people will receive 100 times more than they already
have in this world. That is, they will receive many homes, many
brothers and sisters, many mothers and children and fields.
People will also hurt them because they are obeying God. But
after they die, they will live with God for always. 30But many
people who are very important now will become the least
important. Many who are now the least important people will
become very important.'

20

Jesus tells a story about some workers in a field

1'I will tell you what the Kingdom* of Heaven* is like. The
master of the house went out early in the morning. He wanted
to find some people who would work in his field. He would pay
these workers. 2The master agreed with the workers that he
would pay them one small silver* coin a day. And he sent them
to work in the field.'

3'The master went out again about three hours later. He
saw some other men standing in the market place. They had
nothing to do. 4So the master said to these men, "You also go
and work in my field. I will pay you the right amount of money."
5So the workers went to the master's field.

The master went out again at noon, and again he went out
three hours after that. Both times he sent men to his field to
work. 6Two hours later, he went out again. And he still found
men who were standing there. And they were doing nothing.
The master asked them, "Why are you standing here all day
and you are doing nothing?"

7The men said to the master, "Nobody has asked us to work for
him."

So the master said to them, "You also go and work in my field."

⁸Then the evening came. And the master of the field went to see the man who watched the workers. "Tell the workers that they must come here", the master said to him. "And pay them their money. Begin with the workers who came last. Finish with the workers who came first."

⁹The workers who had come last to work received one small silver* coin each. ¹⁰The workers who had come first to work also received a small silver* coin. They thought that they would receive more than the other workers. ¹¹But when they received their money, they were not happy. And they told the master that they were not happy. ¹²They said to him, "Some of these other workers came last and only worked for one hour. But you have paid them the same as you paid us. And we have worked all day in the hot sun."

¹³Then the master said to one of the workers, "My friend, I am being fair to you. You did agree to work for one day and to receive one small silver* coin. ¹⁴Take your money and go home. I choose to give this last man the same amount of money as I gave to you. ¹⁵It is my money. I can choose what to do with it. I want to be kind and give plenty of money to everyone. You should be happy about this." '

¹⁶Jesus said, 'So, one day, those people who are the least important will be the most important. And those who are most important now will be least important.'

Jesus talks again about how he will die

¹⁷Jesus was going to Jerusalem. They walked along. Then he led his 12 disciples* to a quiet place where he could speak to them alone. ¹⁸'Listen!' he said. 'When we arrive in Jerusalem, someone will help people to take hold of me, the Son of Man. These people will take me to the leaders of the priests* and the teachers of the Law*. These important Jews* will say that I must die. ¹⁹Then these important Jews* will take me. And they will give me to those who are not Jews*. They will laugh

at* me and hit me with a whip*. Then they will kill me on a cross*. After three days, I will come back to life.'

The wife of Zebedee asks Jesus for something

20 Then Zebedee's wife came to see Jesus. She brought her two sons, James and John, with her. She went down on her knees in front of Jesus. She wanted to ask him to do something good for her.

21 'What do you want?' Jesus asked her.

'One day, you will be king and you will rule your kingdom*', she said. 'Then I want one of my two sons to sit at your right side. I want the other son to sit at your left side. Please will you do this?'

22 Jesus replied to James and John. 'You do not understand what you are asking me to do', he said to them. 'Can you have pain and trouble in the same way that I will have pain and trouble?'

'Yes, we can do this', said James and John.

23 Jesus said to them, 'Yes, that is true. You will have pain and trouble in the same way that I will have pain and trouble. But I cannot promise that you will sit at my right side or at my left side. God has chosen who will sit there. He has prepared the places for them.'

24 When the other 10 disciples* heard about this, they were angry with the two brothers. 25 But Jesus asked the 12 men to come near him. 'You know how the rulers of other countries rule', Jesus said. 'They have great power over the people. Their leaders have great authority over them. 26 I do not want you to be like that. The person who wants to be most important person among you must be a servant to the other disciples*. 27 The person who wants to be the most important person must be like the least important servant to everyone. 28 The Son of Man himself came to earth to be a servant to other people. He did not come here to have servants who

would work for him. He came to die so that many people can be free.'

Jesus causes two men to see again

29 When Jesus and his disciples* left Jericho, a large crowd followed him. 30 Now, two men were sitting at the side of the road. These men could not see. But they heard that Jesus was walking along near them. So they shouted, 'Jesus, Son of David, please be kind to us.'

31 The people who were in the crowd were angry with them. And they tried to stop the men shouting. 'Be quiet!' they said. But the men shouted even louder, 'Son of David, please be kind to us.'

32 Jesus stopped walking and he spoke to the two men. 'What do you want me to do for you?' he asked.

33 'Sir', the men replied, 'we want to see again.'

34 Then Jesus felt sorry for the two men. He touched their eyes and immediately the men could see again. So they followed him along the road.

21

Jesus goes into Jerusalem

1 Jesus and his 12 disciples* were coming near to Jerusalem. They came first to the village called Bethphage. They were on the hill called the Hill of Olives*.

2 'Go into the village that is in front of you', Jesus said to two of his disciples*. 'As you go into the village, you will find a donkey* tied there with her young donkey. Undo the ropes* and bring them both here to me.'

3 'Someone may ask you, "Why are you taking the donkeys*?" Say to him, "The Master needs them. He will send them back to you soon." '

4This happened to cause the words that the prophet* had spoken to become true,

  5 'Say to the people in Jerusalem,
  "Look, your king is coming.
  He does not come like someone who thinks that he is
    important.
  And he is riding on a donkey*.
  He is riding on the foal of a donkey*." '

6So the two disciples* went to the village. They did everything that Jesus had asked them to do. 7They brought the donkey* and the young donkey to Jesus. They put their coats on the donkeys*. And then Jesus climbed up and he sat on one of them. 8Many people in the crowd put their coats down on the road. Other people cut down some branches from the trees. And they put these branches down on the road.

9Many people went in front of Jesus and many people followed him. All the people shouted,

  'Welcome! We pray that God will be good to you, the Son of
    David!
  Happy is the king who comes with God's authority.
  Let us say how good is our God in heaven*.'

10When Jesus rode into Jerusalem, everybody in the city was very happy. They were asking each other, 'Who is this man?'

11The people in the crowd replied, 'This is Jesus. He comes from Nazareth in Galilee. He is the prophet* that God promised to send.'

Jesus visits God's Great House

12 Jesus went to the place outside God's Great House. People were buying and selling things there. Jesus caused them all to leave. He pushed over the tables of the men who bought and sold money. He pushed over the seats of the men who sold birds.

¹³ Jesus spoke to them all. He said, 'The prophets* wrote God's words in a book. "My House", God said, "will be a place where people can come to pray ." But you have caused it to be a place where people rob other people.'

¹⁴ People who could not see went to meet Jesus at the place outside God's Great House. People who could not walk very well also went there. And Jesus caused them all to become well. ¹⁵ The important priests* and teachers of the Law* saw all the powerful things that Jesus did. They also saw children in the place outside God's Great House. The children were shouting, 'Welcome! We pray that God will be good to you, Son of David!' All these things caused the important Jews* to become very angry.

¹⁶ They asked Jesus, 'Can you hear what these children are saying?'

'Yes', Jesus replied. 'I am sure that you have read this message from God,

"Babies and children say how important you are.
Their words will be completely beautiful and correct." '

¹⁷ Then Jesus left everyone and he went out of Jerusalem. He stayed that night in Bethany.

Jesus causes a fruit tree to die

¹⁸ The next day, Jesus returned from Bethany to Jerusalem early in the morning. He was hungry. ¹⁹ And while he was walking along, he saw a fruit tree near to the road. He went to look for fruit on it. But there were only leaves on the tree, and no fruit. Jesus said to the tree, 'No fruit will ever grow on you again.' Then, immediately, the tree dried up and it died.

²⁰ The disciples* saw it happen and they were very surprised. And they asked Jesus, 'How did the tree dry up so quickly?'

²¹ 'What I say to you is true', Jesus said to them. 'You must really believe in God. You must believe how powerful God

really is. If you believe this, then you could do the same thing to this fruit tree. And also, you could say to this mountain, "Stand up and throw yourself into the sea." If you said that to the mountain, it would happen. 22 If you really believe, then pray. Ask him to give you something. And he will give you the thing that you ask him for.'

23 Then Jesus returned to the place outside God's Great House. While he was teaching the people, the leaders of the priests* and important Jews* went to him. 'What authority do you have to do these things?' they asked him. 'Tell us. Who gave you the authority to do them?'

24 'I also will ask you something', replied Jesus. 'If you tell me the right answer, then I will answer your question. I will tell you where my authority comes from. 25 John had authority to baptise* people. Did this authority come from God or did a man tell him to do it?' Then all the Jewish* leaders talked to each other about Jesus' question. 'We might say that John's authority came from God', they said. 'But then Jesus will ask us why we did not believe John. 26 We might say that a man gave John his authority. But the people all think that John was a prophet*. We would be afraid that they might attack us.'

27 So the Jewish* leaders answered Jesus. 'We do not know who gave John his authority.'

Jesus said to them, 'And I will not tell you who gave me authority to do these things.'

Jesus tells a story about two sons

28 Jesus said to the important Jews*, 'Tell me what you think about this story. A man had two sons. He went to the older son and said, "Son, go and work in the field today."

29 The older son replied, "I do not want to go and work in the field today." But after he had said that, he decided to go to the field.

30 The man went to his other son and he said the same thing to him. The second son replied, "Yes father, I will go." But then he did not go to work in the field.

31 Now which of the man's sons did what his father wanted?' Jesus asked the important Jews*.

They replied, 'The older son did what his father wanted.'

'What I say to you is true', said Jesus. 'The men who take taxes* will go into the Kingdom* of God before you. Also the women who have sex with men for money will go into the Kingdom* of God before you. 32 I say this because of the way that John came to you. He explained to you the right way to obey God. You did not believe him. But those people who did really bad things believed John. You knew that these people believed him. But, even then, you would not believe John's message. You have done wrong things. But you would not tell God that you were sorry. And you would not obey him.'

Jesus tells a story about a farmer

33 Then Jesus spoke again to the important Jews*. 'Listen to another story that I want to tell you. There was a man who had his own farm. He planted vines* in his field, and then he built a wall round it. He dug a hole in the ground to put the grapes* in. Later, he would make them into wine*. He also made a tall building. From the top of the building, a servant would watch the field.'

35 Then the farmers took hold of the servants. They hit one servant with sticks. They killed another of the servants and they threw stones at the other servant. 36 So the master sent other servants to the field. He sent more servants than the first time. But the farmers did the same thing to these servants also. 37 After that, the master sent his own son to the farmers. He thought that the farmers would be kind to his son.

38The farmers saw the master's son coming. "This is the master's own son", they said to each other. "When our master dies, his son will have this field. So, let us kill the master's son and then we can have the field." 39Then the farmers took hold of the son. They pushed him out of the field and then they killed him.

40One day, the master will return', said Jesus. 'What do you think he will do to those farmers?'

41The important Jews* said to Jesus, 'The master will ask someone to kill those bad people in a bad way. Then he will ask someone else to be the farmers in his field. Those new farmers will give the master the fruit that is for him.'

42Jesus said to them, 'I am sure that you have read this. The prophets* wrote,

> "The people who built the house did not want to use one special stone.
> They thought it had no value.
> Now that stone is the most important stone.
> It makes the corner of the wall strong.
> God did this. And we can see that he did something great."

43I am telling you this because God will take his kingdom* away from you. He will give it to people who will obey God.

44When a person falls on to that stone, he will break his body. When that stone falls on top of someone, it will break him completely.'

45The leaders of the priests* and the Pharisees* heard what Jesus said. They understood that he was speaking against them in his stories. 46They wanted to take hold of Jesus and put him in prison. But the people thought that Jesus was a prophet*. So they did not try to do it because they were afraid of the people.

22

Jesus tells a story about a meal at a marriage

¹Jesus continued to teach the people with stories. ²'I will tell you again what the Kingdom* of Heaven* is like', he said. 'A king prepared to have a special meal for his son when he got married. He sent his servants to prepare a big meal for everyone to eat at the marriage. ³He had asked many people to come. So he sent his servants out to tell them that the meal was ready. But many people refused to come.

⁴So the king then sent out other servants. He said to them, "Please tell this message to all those people that I have asked to come. Say that the master says: 'My servants have prepared the meal. They have killed my large cow and some fat young cows. Everything is ready. Come to the meal at the marriage!' "

⁵But none of the people was interested in the king's message. They went away to do their usual work. One man went to his farm and another man went to his business. ⁶Other people took hold of the king's servants. They hurt them and then they killed them. ⁷The king was very angry and he said to his soldiers, "Go out into the city where these people live. Kill those people who killed my servants. And burn down their city!"

⁸Then the king said to his other servants, "The meal that my servants have prepared for the marriage is ready. But the people that I asked to come had no value. ⁹Go out now to the wide streets in the town. Ask all the people that you meet there to come to the meal. The king has prepared it for his son." ¹⁰Then those servants went out into the streets. And they brought to the king's house all the people that they met. Some were good people and some were bad people. Many people came so that the room for the marriage was full.

11 Then the king came into the room to see all the people. He saw one man who was not wearing the right clothes for a marriage. 12 The king said to the man, "So, how did you come in here, my friend? You are not wearing the right clothes for a marriage." The man did not answer.

13 The king said to his servants, "Tie him up so that he cannot move his hands or his feet. Throw him into the dark place outside. There, people will cry. They will also bite their teeth against each other because they are angry."

14 God asks many people to come under his rule. But he only chooses a few people.'

The Pharisees* ask Jesus about paying taxes*

15 After this, the Pharisees* thought about what they could do. They wanted to ask Jesus difficult questions. They wanted to hear him say something bad about the Roman* ruler. 16 So the Pharisees* sent their own disciples* to Jesus. And they also sent people who were in Herod's group. They all said to Jesus, 'Teacher, we know that you are an honest man. It really is true that you teach the right things about God. It does not matter to you what other people think. It does not matter to you if someone is an important person or not. 17 Here is a question for you, Jesus. Tell us what you think about this. Should we pay our taxes* to the Roman* ruler, called Caesar? Or should we not pay them?'

18 Jesus knew why they had asked him this question. It was because they wanted to do bad things to him. So he said to them, 'You are trying to cause me to say something wrong. You are hypocrites*! 19 Show me the coin that you use for the tax*.' They brought him a coin. 20 Then Jesus asked them, 'Whose picture and name are on the coin?'

21 They replied, 'It is Caesar's picture and Caesar's name.'

So Jesus said to them, 'Give to Caesar the things that are for Caesar. And give to God the things that are for God.'

²²When they heard Jesus' answer, they were very surprised. So they left him and they went away.

The Sadducees* ask Jesus a question

²³On that day, some Sadducees* also came to Jesus. These men did not believe that anyone will live again after his death. The Sadducees* asked Jesus a question.

²⁴'Teacher', they said to Jesus, 'Moses wrote these things for us in the Law*. A woman marries a man. But the man dies before the woman has any children. That man's brother must then marry her. They can have children for the man who died. If they have children, the children will be called the children of the first husband. ²⁵Once, there were seven brothers who lived here. The oldest brother married a woman. Then he died before the woman had any children. ²⁶The next younger brother then married her. And then he also died. So a third brother married this woman. And the same thing happened to all the brothers down to the seventh brother. They all died before the woman had any children. ²⁷After this, the woman also died. ²⁸Now some people say that one day dead people will become alive again. On that day, whose wife will that woman be? She had married all seven of those brothers.'

²⁹Jesus said to the Sadducees*, 'You are wrong. You do not know what God says in his book. You do not know how powerful God is. ³⁰One day, people who are dead will become alive again. But then men and women will not marry. They will be like the angels* in heaven*. They do not marry. ³¹It is true that one day dead people will live again. You have read about what God said to you, ³²"I am the God of Abraham, the God of Isaac and the God of Jacob." God is not God of people who are dead. He is the God of people who are now alive.'

³³The crowd heard this. They were very surprised about what Jesus had told the Sadducees*.

Jesus teaches the Pharisees* about
the most important Law*

34 The Pharisees* heard that Jesus had said these things to the Sadducees*. Now the Sadducees* had stopped asking Jesus any questions. So the Pharisees* met together in one place.

35 One of the Pharisees* was also a teacher of the Law*. He asked Jesus a question. He wanted Jesus to say something wrong. 36 'Teacher', he said to Jesus, 'which of our Laws* is the most important Law* for us to obey?'

37 Jesus replied to the Pharisee*, 'You must completely love the Lord your God. You should love him with all that you are. Love him in all that you think. Love him in all that you do. 38 This is the greatest Law* and the most important of all the Laws*. 39 The second Law* is as important as the first. You must love other people as much as you love yourself. 40 All the Laws* of Moses teach us that. And also all the things that the prophets* teach about God are in these two Laws*.'

Jesus teaches people about the Christ*

41 While the Pharisees* were together with Jesus, he asked them, 42 'What do you think about the Christ*, the special person that God will send to us? Whose Son is he?'

The Pharisees* replied, 'He will be from the family of King David.'

43 Jesus asked them, 'Can you explain this to me then? God's Holy Spirit* told David that the special person from God was called Lord. David says, 44 "The Lord said to my Lord:

'Sit at the important place at my right side.
Remain there until I beat your enemies down to the ground.
I will put them down like a place to rest your feet.' "

45 So', Jesus said, 'we know that David calls this special person, "Lord". So how can he be a man from the family of King David?'

⁴⁶Nobody could answer the question that Jesus asked. After this, everyone was afraid to ask Jesus any more questions.

23

Jesus talks about dangerous teachers

¹After that, Jesus spoke to the crowd and to his disciples*. ²'The teachers of the Law* and the Pharisees* have authority to explain the Law* of Moses. ³You must obey everything that they teach you. But you must not do the same things that they do. They teach you what the Law* of Moses is. But then they themselves do not obey these rules. ⁴The rules that they give you are hard to obey. They are like heavy luggage, which they tie on your shoulders. But they will not help you even a little bit to carry these heavy things.'

⁵'They do everything so that the people will see them. They make their phylacteries very large and they make their tassels long.'

⁶'But the teachers of the Law* and the Pharisees* like to sit in the important places at special meals. They also sit in the important places in the buildings where people meet to pray. ⁷They like people to call them "My teacher." In the market place, they want many people to speak to them as people would speak to an important person.

⁸You all believe in God. You have only one teacher. So nobody should call another person, "My teacher".'

⁹'Do not call another person in the world "Father". You have only one Father, and he lives in heaven*.'

¹⁰'Do not call each other "Leader". You have only one leader. And he is the Christ* that God will send to you. ¹¹The person among you who is most important will be your servant. ¹²Someone may think that he himself is very important. But God will cause that person to become the least important person. Someone may think that he is the least

important person. But God will cause that person to become very important.'

Jesus tells the teachers of the Law* and the Pharisees* that they are hypocrites*

13 Jesus spoke to the teachers of the Law* and the Pharisees*. 'Trouble will come to you', he said. 'You are hypocrites*! You have taken away the key that opens a door. It is the door to where people learn about God. They want to go in and find out how God rules. You yourselves will not go into the Kingdom* of Heaven*. Nor will you let other people go in who want to.'

14 'Trouble will come to you, teachers of the Law* and Pharisees*. You are hypocrites*! You take things away from women whose husbands have died. You want people to think good things about you, so you pray for a long time. God will punish* you more than people who have not done these things.'

15 'Trouble will come to you, teachers of the Law* and Pharisees*. You are hypocrites*. You travel across land and across the sea. You do this to make one person believe what you believe. Then when he does believe it, he is even worse than you. He does more bad things than you do. So you cause him to go to hell*.

16 Trouble will come to you, teachers. You cannot see, but you are teaching people which way to go.'

'You say this to people. "Maybe you make a promise like this. 'I promise by the name of God's Great House'. Then you do not need to do what you promised to do. But then you make a different promise. You say, 'I promise by the gold on God's Great House.' Then you must do what you promised to do." 17 You are like a man who cannot see. And you are fools. I will tell you which of these two things is most important. The gold on God's Great House is not important. But God's Great House is really important and it makes the gold important. 18 You also teach the people this: "Maybe you make a promise like this. 'I promise by the name of the special table in God's House.'

Then you do not need to do what you promised to do. But then you make a different promise. You say, 'I promise by the gift on the special table.' Then you should do what you promised to do." [19] You are like people who cannot see. You are fools. I will tell you which of these two things is most important. The gift on the special table is not important. But the special table is really important and it makes the gift important. [20] Maybe a person makes a promise like this. He says, "I promise by the name of the special table in God's Great House". Then he is making a promise to God. It is God's table. All the gifts on it are for God. [21] Perhaps a person says this. "I promise by the name of God's Great House". Then he is making a promise to God. It is his House with everything in it. [22] Perhaps a person says, "I promise by the sky above". The sky is God's. It is the place where he sits. And he rules there.'

[23] 'Teachers of the Law* and Pharisees*, trouble is coming to you. You are hypocrites*! You only obey the very small matters in the Law*. You grow special small plants to use when you cook. You give to God one part out of ten parts of these plants. This is a small matter in the Law* which you obey. But the more important parts of the Law* you forget to obey. It is important to be good and kind to other people. It is also important to believe and to obey God. You should do all these important things as well as the other things that are not so important. [24] You are like a man who cannot see, but you are showing other people the way. You take a small fly out of your cup so that you do not drink it. But you do not see the large animal that is swimming in it.'

[25] 'Teachers of the Law* and Pharisees*, trouble is coming to you. You are hypocrites*! You are like someone who is careful to wash the outside of a cup and a plate. The inside of the cup and plate are also dirty. But you do not wash that. The dirt is like the things you do. You want more things than you should have. You hurt people to get what you want. [26] Pharisees*, you are like men who cannot see. You must first clean the inside of the cup and plate. Then the outside will also be clean.

27Teachers of the Law* and Pharisees*, trouble is coming to
you. You are hypocrites*! You bury dead people in holes in
the rock. You put white paint outside the holes on the stones.
You are like these white stones outside these holes. They look
beautiful on the outside, but they are full of the bones of dead
people and bad things. 28 You are the same as these holes.
Other people look at you. They think that you obey God. But
really, you are hypocrites* and you do many very bad things.

29Teachers of the Law* and Pharisees*, things will be bad
for you. You are hypocrites*! You build beautiful places. You
bury the prophets* in these places after they have died. You
cause the places where you have buried good people to be
beautiful. 30 You say, "Our ancestors* killed God's prophets*. If
we had lived at that time, we would not have helped them to
kill the prophets*." 31 So you are speaking against yourselves.
You are saying that you are the sons of these people. These
people killed God's prophets*. 32 Finish then the work that your
ancestors* began!

33 You are like snakes, and like a family of dangerous snakes.
You will not be able to run away. I am sure that God will judge*
you. And he will send you to hell*. 34 So I tell you this. I will
send prophets* to you. I will also send people who know many
things. And I will send people to teach you. But you will kill
some of these people. You will kill some of them on a cross*. In
the places where you meet to pray, you will hit some of them
with whips*. They will run from one town to another town, but
you will follow them. 35 Let me tell you why I send these people
to you. Because of the things that you will do, God will punish*
you. You will receive the punishment* for the murder of Abel.
He was a good man. You killed many other good men. You also
murdered Zechariah, the son of Berechiah. He also was a good
man, but your leaders killed him. He died between God's Great
House and God's special table.'

36 'What I am saying is true. God will punish* all you people
who are alive today. He will do this because of all the bad
things that your ancestors* did.

37Oh, you people who live in Jerusalem! Oh, you people who live in Jerusalem! When God sends prophets* to you, you throw stones at them. And you kill them. Many times, I have wanted to bring all of you near to me. A bird brings all her little birds together and she covers them with her body. But you would not let me take care* of you like that. 38So listen! Soon nobody will remain here to live in this place. This is true. 39One day you will say, "Happy is the man whom God sends here with his authority." But you will not see me again until you say that.'

24

Jesus talks about things that would happen soon

1Jesus left God's Great House, and his disciples* came to him. They began to talk to Jesus about the buildings of God's Great House. 2So Jesus said to them, 'Yes, you can see all these beautiful buildings now. But what I say is true. The day is coming soon when enemies will completely destroy them. They will not leave one stone on top of another stone. They will throw every stone down from the buildings.'

3Jesus then sat on the hill called the Hill of Olives*. While he was alone, his disciples* came to him. 'Tell us when this will happen', they said to him. 'What will we see just before you return? What will show that God will soon end the world?'

4Jesus said, 'Be careful and watch. Some people will tell you things that are not true. But do not believe them. 5Many people will come and say, "I am the Christ*." Many other people will believe that this is true. 6You will hear the noise of wars near where you are. You will hear about people who are fighting wars in places a long way away. Do not be afraid. These things must happen first, but it is not yet the end of everything. 7People in one country will attack the people in another country. Kings and their people will fight against other kings and their people. The ground will move in many different places. Some people will not have any food to eat because the plants for food will not grow. 8 These things will be like the first pains that start before a baby is born.

9 Then people will take hold of you because you believe in me. They will punish* some of you and they will kill some of you. Some people in every country will hate* you because you obey me. 10 At that time, many people who believe in me will stop believing. They will put some of those who follow me in the power of their rulers. And they will hate* all those who still follow me. 11 Also at that time, many people will say that they are prophets*. This will not be true, but many people will believe them. 12 More and more people everywhere will be doing very bad things. Because of this many people will no longer love each other in the way that they did. 13 But you must never stop believing in me. Then God will save you. 14 People will tell the good news about the Kingdom* to people all over the world. People will know that the message is true. And they will tell it to other people in every country in the world. Only then will God cause the world to come to an end.

15 Long ago Daniel, the prophet*, wrote in God's book. He said that one day people would put something very bad in God's Great House. They would put it in the special place for God. This will then happen. At that time, you must understand what Daniel wrote. 16 When you see this very bad thing, people in Judea must run to the hills. They must run so that their enemies do not catch them.

17 A man who is on the roof of his house must not go down into his house. He must not waste time to fetch anything in his home to take with him.'

18 'People who are outside the city in their fields must not go back home. They must not waste any time. So they must not even go to fetch their coats. 19 Those days will be bad for women who have a baby inside them! And those days will be bad for those women who have little babies! 20 You must pray to God and say, "Please do not let these things happen in winter. Please do not let them happen on the day when we

rest." ²¹People will have great troubles. From the time that God made the world, nothing so bad has ever happened. After this bad time has finished, it will never ever be so bad again. ²²God will make this time of great trouble shorter. If he did not do that, there would be nobody still alive. God will cause this time of trouble to be shorter to help the people that he has chosen. ²³Someone may say to you, "Look, here is the Christ*." Or they may say, "Look, there is the Christ*." When they say that, do not believe them. ²⁴Some people will say to you, "I am the special man. God has sent me." Other people will come and they will say, "I am a prophet* of God." None of the things that these people say is true. They will do powerful things that people cannot usually do. They will be trying to cause people to believe that their words are true. They will even try to cause the people that God has chosen to believe in them. ²⁵So be careful and watch out! I have told you about all these things before they happen.

²⁶Some people may say to you, "Look, the Christ* is out there in the desert*." But you must not go out to see who is there. Some people may say to you, "Look, the Christ* is in there in that secret room." You must not believe these people. ²⁷Lightning* shines quickly and it lights up the whole of the sky. It will be like that when the Son of Man returns. ²⁸Big birds that eat meat arrive together. They all arrive where there is a dead body.'

²⁹'Then after all these bad things have happened,

"The sun will become dark.
The moon will stop shining.
Stars will fall down out of the sky,
and God will cause all the powerful things in the sky to
move from their usual places."

³⁰Then people will see something powerful in the sky. This will show them that the Son of Man is coming. All the people in the world will weep because they are very sad. Then people will see the Son of Man coming down in the clouds. He will be very

powerful. He will be great and very beautiful. [31] The sound of a loud trumpet* will go out. The Son of Man will send out God's angels* in every direction. They will bring together all the people that God has chosen from every part of the world.'

Jesus tells a story about a fig* tree

[32] 'I will tell you a story about a fig* tree. You can learn something from what the tree does. When the new branches on the tree start to grow, the leaves appear. Then you know that the summer is coming soon. [33] In the same way, you will see all these things happen. Then you will know that the Son of Man is coming soon. He is like someone at the door who is ready to come in. [34] The things that I say to you are true. The people who are living then will see all these things. They will not die before all these things have happened. [35] One day, the earth and the sky will finish. But my words will never finish.'

Nobody will know when the Son of Man will return to the world

[36] 'Nobody knows the day or the time when all these things will happen. Even the angels* in heaven* do not know. Even God's Son does not know. Only God the Father knows when they will happen. [37] It was the same as this when Noah was alive. And it will be the same again when the Son of Man returns. [38] In the days before the rain came, people were eating. People were drinking. Men married women and women married men. They did all these things until the day that Noah climbed into his big boat. [39] The people did not know what would happen. Then rain fell for a long time and all these people died in the deep water. When the Son of Man returns, it will be the same. People will not know that it is going to happen at that moment. [40] At that time, it will be like this. Two men will be working in a field. God will take one man away, but he will leave the other man behind. [41] Two women will be working together in the same place. God will take one woman away, but he will leave the other woman behind.'

⁴²'Be careful and watch! You do not know the day or time when your Master will come. ⁴³You can be sure about this. The master of the house did not know at what time of night a man would come to rob him. If the master had known the time, he would have watched his house more carefully. Then the man would not have robbed his house. ⁴⁴So you must also be ready. It will be a surprise for you when the Son of Man returns.'

Jesus tells a story about two servants

⁴⁵Then Jesus finished teaching them. 'I will tell you about a good servant. His master knows that he will obey. He knows how to do everything well. The master chooses him to rule over all his other servants. He will give everyone the food that they need each day. ⁴⁶The master will come home. And he will see this servant obeying all that he told him to do. So the master will be kind to his servant. ⁴⁷What I say is true. The master will then ask the servant to rule over everything in his house. ⁴⁸But perhaps the servant is bad and he says to himself, "My master will not come yet." ⁴⁹So, he begins to hit the other servants. He hits both the men and the women. He eats too much. He also drinks with drunks.'

⁵⁰'Then the master of that servant will come home and he will surprise the servant. He did not think that his master would come home on that day or at that time. ⁵¹Then the master will punish* him a lot. He will put the servant with those people who do not obey him. The people in that place will cry. And they will bite their teeth together because they are angry.'

25

Jesus tells a story about ten young women

¹'I will tell you again what the Kingdom* of Heaven* is like. There were ten young women who were going to a marriage. They took their lamps* with them and they went to meet the bridegroom*. ²Five of these young women were silly. They were not careful about what they were doing. Five of these

young women understood well. They were careful about what they were doing. ³The silly young women took their lamps* with them, but they did not take any extra oil with them. ⁴The other five young women took jars of oil with them. These young women were careful about what they were doing. ⁵The bridegroom* did not come for a long time. So all the young women became tired, and they went to sleep.

⁶In the middle of the night, someone shouted out, "The bridegroom* is coming. Come out to meet him."

⁷The ten young women woke up. Then they got up and they looked at their lamps*. They tried to make their lamps* work well. ⁸The five young women who had not brought extra oil said to the other five young women, "Give us some of your oil, because our lamps* are not burning well."

⁹The careful young women who had extra oil replied, "If we did that, then there would not be enough oil for all of us. You must go instead to the people who sell oil. You must buy some oil for your lamps*." '

¹⁰'So these five women went to buy some oil. While they were away, the bridegroom* arrived. He would soon marry. The five women who understood well were ready. They went with him into the house. Here the servants had prepared the meal for the marriage. Then the servants shut the door.

¹¹Later, the five silly women also came to the house. They said, "Sir, Sir, please open the door for us."

¹²But he replied, "What I say is true. I do not know you." '

¹³Then Jesus said, 'So you must watch well. You do not know on what day or at what time I will come.'

Jesus tells a story about three servants

¹⁴'I will tell you again what the Kingdom* of Heaven* is like. A man was going on a journey. Before he went away, he asked his servants to come to him. He said to them, "Take care* of

all my money and all my things for me." 15 The master gave one servant 5000 gold coins. He gave another servant 2000 gold coins, and to another servant he gave 1000 gold coins. He gave to each servant what he would be able to use well. Then the master went away on his journey.'

16 'The servant who had received 5000 gold coins went out immediately. He bought and sold things with the money. This servant got 5000 more gold coins. 17 The servant who had received 2000 gold coins also went out immediately. He also bought and sold things with the money. This servant got 2000 more gold coins. 18 The servant who had received 1000 gold coins did something different. He went outside and he dug a hole in the ground. He buried the money that his master had given him.

19 After a long time, the master came home. He asked the servants to come to him. He wanted to know how much money they had now. 20 The servant who had received 5000 gold coins came to his master. The servant said to him, "Master, you gave me 5000 gold coins. And now I have another 5000 gold coins."

21 The master said to this servant, "You are a good servant; you have done really well. You were careful with a little money. I will give you much more money to use. I am really happy about this and I want you to be happy with me."

22 The servant who had received 2000 gold coins also came to his master. The servant said to him, "Master, you gave me 2000 gold coins. And now I have another two thousand gold coins."

23 The master said to his servant, "You are a good servant; you have done really well. You were careful with a little money. I will give you much more to use. I am really happy about this and I want you to be happy with me."

24 The servant who had received 1000 gold coins also came to his master. The servant said to him, "Master, I know what

you are like. You ask people to do things all the time. You get seeds back from the ground, which you did not plant. You get fruit from trees that you did not plant. 25 I was afraid of you, so I buried your money in the ground. See, here it is. You can have it back again."

26 The master said to him, "You are a bad and lazy servant. You said that you know about me. I get seeds back that I did not plant. I get fruit from trees that I did not plant. And you knew all that. 27 You should have put the money into the bank. Then, when I came home, I could have received my money back from the bank again, with extra money also."

28 Then the master said to his other servants, "Take the 1000 gold coins from this man. Give them to the man who now has 10 thousand coins." 29 Then the master said, "What I say is true. I will give more to every person who already has something. He will have much more than he needs. Another person has almost nothing. I will take away even the small amount that he has. 30 This servant cannot work for me any longer. So you can throw him into a dark place outside. People will weep there. And they will bite their teeth together because they are angry." '

God judges* everybody

31 'When I, the Son of Man return, I will be powerful and great and important and beautiful. All the angels* will come with me. I will sit on my seat as king. 32 All the people in the world will be together in front of me. I will put them into two groups. I will do it in the same way that a shepherd puts his sheep and goats into two groups. 33 He puts the sheep on his right side and the goats on his left side.'

34 'The king will say to those people who are on his right side, "Come here. My Father has given you good things. He has prepared a place for you in his Kingdom*. From the time that God made the world, he made a place ready for you." 35 Then the king said to them, "I was hungry and you gave me some

food to eat. I needed to drink and you gave me some water.
I was alone and you asked me to come to your home. 36 I did
not have enough clothes and you gave me some more to wear.
I was ill and you took care* of me. I was in prison and you
came to visit me there."

37 The people who did good things will speak to him. "Master,
when did we see that you were hungry? And when did we give
you some food? When did we see that you needed to drink?
And when did we give you some water? 38 When did we see
that you were alone? And when did we ask you to come to our
home? When did we see that you did not have enough clothes?
And when did we give you some more clothes? 39 When did we
see you that you were ill? And when did we take care* of you?
When did we know that you were in prison? And when did we
come to visit you?"

40 The king will answer them, "What I say to you is true. You
did all these things to help people. They were not important
people, but they were my friends. If you helped them, then
you also helped me."

41 Then the king will say to those people who are at his left side,
"Go away from me. God has said that bad things will happen to
you. God has prepared a fire that will burn for always. He has
prepared it for Satan* and those who help him. You will also
go into that fire." 42 Then the king said to them, "I was hungry
but you did not give me any food to eat. I needed to drink but
you did not give me anything. 43 I was alone but you did not
ask me to come to your home. I did not have enough clothes
but you did not give me anything to wear. I was ill but you did
not take care* of me. I was in prison but you did not come to
visit me."

44 Then these other people will speak to the king. "Master,
when did we see you hungry, or needing something to drink?
Or when did we see you alone, or without enough clothes? Or
when did we see you ill, or in prison and we did not give you
any help?"

45 Then the king will reply, "What I say to you is true. You did not do these things for people. They were not important people. But when you did not help them, you also did not help me."

46 These people who did not help other people will go away. God will punish* them for always. But those good people who obey God will live for always.'

26

Those who are against Jesus want to take hold of him

1 When Jesus finished saying these things, he said to his disciples*. 2 'Now you know that after two days we will eat the Passover* meal. Then those people who are against me will put me into the power of the rulers. They will fix me to a cross*.'

3 Then the leaders of the priests* and the important Jews* met together in the house of Caiaphas. Caiaphas was the most important priest* in Jerusalem. 4 They talked about the best way to take hold of Jesus. But they did not want other people to know about their idea. 5 They said to each other, 'We do not want to take hold of him during the Passover*. The people may fight against us if we do that.'

A woman pours oil that has a beautiful smell on Jesus' head

6 Then Jesus went to Bethany and he visited Simon at his house. At one time, Simon had had an illness of the skin.

7 While Jesus was eating a meal, a woman came into the house. She brought a small stone jar with her. The jar contained very expensive oil. It had a very nice smell. She poured the oil over Jesus' head.

8 Jesus' disciples* saw what the woman had done. They became angry and they said, 'This woman should not have

wasted the oil. ⁹She could have sold it for a lot of money. Then she could have given the money to poor people.'

¹⁰Jesus knew what his disciples* were saying. So he said to them, 'Do not be angry with her. Stop speaking to her like that. She has done a beautiful thing for me. ¹¹You will always have poor people with you. But I will not always be with you. ¹²She poured oil over my body to prepare it. So, now my body is ready for people to bury me. ¹³What I say to you is true. Everywhere people will tell this good news. They will also tell about what this woman did. Then other people will think about her because of what she did.'

Judas Iscariot promises to sell Jesus for money

¹⁴Judas Iscariot was one of Jesus' 12 disciples*. He went to see the important priests* ¹⁵and he asked them, 'How much money will you give me if I help you to take hold of Jesus?' The priests* gave Judas 30 silver* coins. ¹⁶Judas then waited for the right moment to help them take hold of Jesus.

Jesus eats his last meal with his 12 disciples*

¹⁷It was now the first day of the Passover*. On this day, people ate bread that they had made without yeast* in it. Jesus disciples* came to talk to him. 'Where do you want us to prepare the Passover* meal for you to eat?' they said to him.

¹⁸Jesus replied, 'Go to a certain man in the city and say to him, "The teacher says: This is the moment that God has prepared for me. I will eat the Passover* meal with my disciples* in your house." ' ¹⁹So Jesus' disciples* did what he had asked them to do. And they prepared the Passover* meal.

²⁰That evening, Jesus and the 12 disciples* sat down to eat the Passover* meal together. ²¹While they were eating, Jesus said, 'What I say is true. One of you will help the Jewish* rulers to take hold of me.'

²²They were very sad about what Jesus had said. Each one of them said to Jesus, 'Teacher, I am sure that you do not mean me.'

²³Jesus said to them 'It is the man who is putting the end of his bread into the same dish as me. That man will help the Jewish* rulers to take hold of me.'

²⁴'The Son of Man will die in the way that God's prophets* wrote. But trouble will come to the man who causes this to happen. He should not have helped the rulers to take hold of me. It would be better for that man if he had never come into this world.'

²⁵It was Judas who would help the Jewish* rulers. But he said to Jesus, 'Teacher, it cannot be me who will do this.' 'Yes, it is you who will do this', Jesus replied to him.

²⁶While Jesus and his disciples* were eating, he took a loaf of bread. He thanked God for it and then he broke the bread into pieces. He then gave it to each of them and he said, 'Take this bread and eat it. This bread is my body.'

²⁷Then Jesus took a cup. He thanked God for the wine* in the cup. Then he gave it to them and each disciple* drank from the cup. ²⁸'This wine* is my blood', he said. 'This is the new promise between God and his people. When I die, my blood will come out. Then God can forgive* people for all the wrong things that they have done. ²⁹I am telling you this. I will not drink wine* again until I drink it with you again in my Father's kingdom*.'

³⁰Then Jesus and his disciples* sang a song to God. Then they all went out to the Hill of Olives*.

Jesus tells Peter what will happen

³¹Then Jesus spoke to his disciples*. 'Tonight, you will all run away and you will stop believing in me. The prophets* wrote this down:

"I will kill the man who takes care* of the sheep.
Then all the sheep that he had will run away to
    different places."

32 But after I die, God will cause me to become alive again.
Then I will go before you to Galilee.'

33 Peter said to Jesus, 'Even if everyone else runs away, I will
not leave you.'

34 Jesus replied to Peter, 'What I say is true. Tonight, you will
say three times that you do not know me. This will happen
before the rooster* makes a noise for the first time in
the morning.'

35 But Peter said, 'Jesus, I will never tell anyone that I do not
know you. Even if that means that I must die with you.' All the
other disciples* said the same thing.

Jesus prays in the garden called Gethsemane on the Hill of Olives*

36 Then they arrived at a large garden called Gethsemane.
Jesus said to the disciples* who were with him, 'Sit here while
I go over there to pray.' 37 Jesus then took Peter and the two
sons of Zebedee with him. He became very sad and troubled
in his mind. 38 'I am very sad. I could die because I feel so sad.
Please wait here and watch with me', Jesus said to them.

39 Jesus went a short way in front of them. He went down on
his knees with his face on the ground. He prayed, 'Father, if
it is possible, please save me from this time of great pain. But
Father, do not give me what I want. But give me what you
want for me.'

40 Jesus returned and he found the disciples*. They were
sleeping. He said to Peter, 'Simon, you are asleep! You could
not stay awake with me for even one hour! 41 You must stay
awake and pray. God can help you, so that you will not do the
wrong thing. You really want to do the right thing, but you are
too weak to stay awake.'

⁴²Jesus went away a second time and he prayed again. 'My Father, if you want, you can take away this pain. If it is not possible to save me from this time of great pain, then I want to obey you.'

⁴³Jesus returned again to them. He saw that they were sleeping. They could not keep their eyes open. ⁴⁴So Jesus went away again and he prayed a third time. He said the same words to God.

⁴⁵When he returned to them, he said, 'You should not be sleeping and resting. You have slept enough. The time has come for me to have much pain. Look! Someone will now help bad men to take hold of me. ⁴⁶Stand up now, because it is time to meet them. Look! Here is the man who will help them to take hold of me.'

The soldiers take hold of Jesus

⁴⁷While Jesus was still speaking, Judas arrived. He was one of Jesus' disciples*. A crowd also appeared with him. They were all carrying long sharp knives and heavy sticks. The important priests*, the teachers of the Law* and the important Jews* had sent these people with Judas. ⁴⁸Now, Judas would help the rulers of the Jews* to take hold of Jesus. He had told the people, 'I will kiss one of the men. He is the man. Take hold of him.' ⁴⁹Judas went immediately to Jesus when they arrived. 'Teacher', he said to him. Then he kissed Jesus.

⁵⁰Jesus said to Judas, 'My friend, you must do what you have come here to do.'

Then the crowd of men came and they took hold of Jesus. ⁵¹Then one of Jesus' disciples* put out his hand and he took hold of his long sharp knife. He hit the servant of the most important priest* with it and he cut off the servant's ear.

⁵²Then Jesus said to the man, 'Put your long sharp knife away in its place. Some people use a long sharp knife to kill. They will die. Someone will kill them with a long sharp knife. ⁵³You

should know that I could ask my Father to help me. He would immediately send more than 12 large groups of angels* to fight for me. ⁵⁴They would save me. But then everything that God said in his book would not happen. And the prophets* have said how all these things must happen.'

⁵⁵Then Jesus spoke to the crowd. 'You have come out here with sharp knives and heavy sticks to take hold of me', he said. 'So you must believe that I am leading people to fight against the rulers. That is how you would take hold of a man like that. I was with you every day in the place outside God's Great House when I was teaching. But you did not take hold of me then. ⁵⁶The prophets* wrote down that all this would happen to me. Now it has become true.' Then all of Jesus' disciples* ran away and left him.

Jesus stands in front of all the important rulers

⁵⁷Then those men who had taken hold of Jesus took him to Caiaphas's house. Caiaphas was the most important priest*. The teachers of the Law* and the important Jews* were meeting together there with Caiaphas.

⁵⁸Peter followed the men who were taking Jesus to the house of the most important priest*. But he was not very near to them. When everyone went into the place outside Caiaphas's house, Peter went in too. He sat down with the police who worked in God's Great House. He wanted to see what would happen.

⁵⁹The leaders of the priests* and the important rulers wanted people to say things about Jesus that were not true. They wanted to kill Jesus. ⁶⁰Many people did come. And they said things about Jesus that were not true. But still they could not find a reason to kill Jesus. Then two men said, ⁶¹'We heard this man say, "I can destroy God's Great House and in 3 days I can build it again." '

⁶²Then Caiaphas stood up in front of everybody and he said to Jesus, 'Will you not reply? These people have said that you

have done many bad things. What do you say about this?' 63 But Jesus did not say anything.

And so Caiaphas said, 'I use God's authority to say to you, "Tell us what is true." Are you the Christ*? Are you the Son of God?'

64 'I am', Jesus replied. 'And you will all see the Son of Man. He will be sitting at the right side of the Most Powerful God in the most important place. You will also see him coming to earth. And he will be riding on the clouds.'

65 Caiaphas tore his coat. 'Jesus spoke against God. We do not need anyone else to tell us about him', he said. 'You have heard him speak against God. 66 What have you decided to do with him?'

'Jesus must die because of the things that he has said', they replied.

67 Then some of the men began to send water from their mouths into Jesus' face. They also hit him with their fists, 68 and they said, 'Tell us who hit you! If you were a prophet*, you could certainly do that!' They also hit him with their open hands.

Peter says three times that he does not know Jesus

69 Now, while all these things were happening, Peter was still sitting outside the house. One of the girls who worked for most important priest* went to talk to him. 'You were also with Jesus, the man from Galilee', she said.

70 Peter said in front of everyone who was there, 'That is not true. I do not know what you are talking about.'

71 Peter then walked to the gate, and another girl saw him. This girl said to the people who were standing there, 'This man was with Jesus, the man from Nazareth.'

⁷²Peter answered everyone again. 'I promise that I do not know that man from Nazareth. I will speak God's name to promise that.'

⁷³After a little while, other people who were standing at the gate spoke to Peter. 'We are sure that you are one of the friends of that man from Nazareth. We know this because you also speak like people who live in Galilee.'

⁷⁴Peter said to them, 'I do not know the man from Nazareth. If this is not true, then God should punish* me!'

Immediately after Peter said this, the rooster* made a noise. ⁷⁵Then Peter remembered that Jesus had said to him, 'Tonight you will say three times that you do not know me. After that, the rooster* will make a noise.' So Peter went outside the house alone. He had a very troubled mind and he began to weep a lot.

27

The important Jews* take Jesus to stand in front of Pilate

¹Early the next morning, all the leaders of the priests* and the important Jews* talked together. They decided to ask the Roman* rulers to kill Jesus. ²They tied Jesus' hands and feet and then they led him away to Pilate's house. The soldiers put Jesus under the authority of Pilate, the ruler.

Judas dies

³Judas heard that the Jews* had asked the Roman* rulers to kill Jesus. Judas had told the Jews* where Jesus was. Now he was very sorry about what he had done. So he took back the 30 valuable coins to the leaders of the priests* and the important Jews*. ⁴Judas said to them, 'I have done the wrong thing. I helped you to take hold of a man who has done nothing wrong.'

They replied to Judas, 'That is not important to us. That is your problem.'

5 Judas threw the money down on the floor in God's Great House. Then he went away. He hung himself from a rope* so that he died.

6 The leaders of the priests* picked up the coins. They said, 'We used this money to catch and kill a man. So it is against our Law* to now use this same money for God's Great House.' 7 They talked together. And they decided to use the money to buy a field. They would use this field to bury foreign people who died in the city. The man who once had this field had made pots and jars out of soil*.

8 After this, the field was called 'The Field of Blood'. And it is still called that until today. 9 So the words of the prophet* Jeremiah became true. He had said a long time before, 'Then they took the 30 silver* coins. 10 This was how much money the people of Israel* had agreed to pay for him. They used this money to buy a field from a man who made pots. God said that I must do this.' When the leaders of the priests* bought the field, all these things happened.

Pilate asks Jesus some questions

11 At that time, Jesus stood in front of the Roman* ruler. Pilate asked Jesus, 'Are you the king of the Jews*?' Jesus replied, 'Yes, it is as you say.'

12 The leaders of the priests* and the important Jews* told Pilate that Jesus had done many bad things. Jesus did not answer them. 13 So then, Pilate said to Jesus, 'These man say that you have done many bad things. You can hear what they are saying.' 14 But Jesus did not answer Pilate. He did not say anything about any of the bad things that the men were talking about. Pilate was very surprised about this.

15 Each year at the time for the Passover* meal, Pilate let one person come out of the prison. The people could choose which

person should be free. ¹⁶At that time, there was a man called Barabbas in prison. Everyone knew about what he had done. ¹⁷Then the crowd came together at Pilate's house. Pilate asked them, 'Do you want me to let Barabbas come out of the prison? Or do you want me to let Jesus out instead? Jesus is called the Christ*.' ¹⁸Pilate knew very well why the rulers of the Jews* had given Jesus to him. They did not like the way that the people listened to Jesus. Many people listened to Jesus more than to their rulers.

¹⁹Pilate was deciding what to do. Then his wife sent him a message. She said, 'Do not do anything to that man. He is a good man and he has done nothing wrong. Last night, when I was sleeping, I had a dream about him. The dream made me very anxious*.'

²⁰But the leaders of the priests* and the important Jews* talked to the people. 'You must ask Pilate to let Barabbas come out of the prison', they said. 'Ask Pilate to kill Jesus.'

²¹Pilate asked the people again, 'Which of these two men should come out of the prison?' The people answered, 'Barabbas.'

²²Then Pilate asked the people, 'What then should I do with Jesus, who is called the Christ*?' The people all shouted, 'Kill him! Kill him on a cross*.'

²³So Pilate said, 'Why should I kill him? What bad things has he done?'

But the people were shouting many times even louder, 'Kill him on a cross*! Kill him on a cross*!'

²⁴Then Pilate knew that he could not do anything to make them quiet. He thought that the people would start to fight his soldiers. So, Pilate took a dish of water and he washed his hands in front of the people. He said, 'It is not because of me that this man will die. You have caused it to happen.'

25 All the people answered Pilate, 'We and our children will answer to God. He can punish* us, if we have done the wrong thing.'

26 Then Pilate sent Barabbas out of the prison. Pilate said to the soldiers, 'Hit Jesus with a whip*. Then fix him to a cross*.'

27 Then Pilate's soldiers took Jesus into a large room in the ruler's house. All the other soldiers in their group were there. 28 They removed Jesus' clothes from him, and they put a dark red coat on him instead. 29 They used plants with sharp branches and they made a crown for him. Then they put it on his head. And they put a long stick in his right hand. They went down on their knees in front of him. They laughed* at him and they said, 'Welcome! You are the King of the Jews*. We go down on our knees in front of you. We hope that you will live for a long time.'

30 Then the soldiers sent water from their mouths into Jesus' face. They took the stick and they hit Jesus on his head with it again and again. 31 After they had finished laughing* at him, they removed the dark red coat. And they put Jesus' own clothes back on him. Then they led him to the place where they would kill him. They would fix him to a cross* made out of wood.

The soldiers kill Jesus on a cross*

32 On the way to that place, they took hold of a man called Simon. He was walking past Jesus and the soldiers. He came from the city called Cyrene. The Roman* soldiers said to Simon, 'Carry this cross*!' Then they pushed him to it. 33 The soldiers led Jesus to the place that is called Golgotha. (Golgotha means the place of a skull.)

34 The soldiers tried to give Jesus some wine* to drink. They had put something like medicine in it. Jesus tasted it, but he would not drink it. 35 Then the Roman* soldiers fixed Jesus on to the cross* and they took his clothes. They played a game among themselves. They did this to find out who would receive

each piece of his clothes. ³⁶Then the soldiers sat down and they watched Jesus carefully. ³⁷Above his head they fixed a notice. They had written on it the reason why they were killing him. The words on the notice were, 'This man is Jesus, the king of the Jews*.' ³⁸Then the soldiers also fixed two other men to crosses*. Those men had robbed people. One man was at Jesus' right side, and one man was at his left side. ³⁹Those people who walked past Jesus said bad things to him. They moved their heads from one side to the other side while they looked at him. ⁴⁰And they said, 'You said that you could destroy God's Great House. You said that in three days you could build it again. If you really are the Son of God, save yourself. Come down from the cross*.'

⁴¹The leaders of the priests* and the teachers of the Law* and the important Jews* were all laughing* at him too. ⁴²'This man saved other people, but he cannot save himself. He says that he is the king of Israel*. If he came down from the cross* now, then we would believe in him. ⁴³He believes in God. So if God wants him, let God save him now. He did say that he is the Son of God.' ⁴⁴Then the two men on crosses* next to Jesus said the same bad things to him.

Jesus dies

⁴⁵It was now about noon. The whole country became dark for three hours. ⁴⁶About three hours after noon, Jesus shouted with a loud voice. He said, 'Eloi, Eloi, lama sabachthani?' That means, 'My God, my God, why have you left me alone?'

⁴⁷Some people were standing near to Jesus. They heard what he had shouted. And they said to each other, 'He is shouting to Elijah the prophet*.'

⁴⁸One of these people ran quickly and he brought a piece of soft material. He poured wine* that was not sweet on it. And then he put it on the end of a stick. He lifted it up to Jesus so that he could drink the wine* from it. ⁴⁹The other people said,

'Wait a moment and watch. We will see if Elijah comes. He might save Jesus.'

50 Then Jesus shouted again with a loud voice. And after that, he died.

51 At that moment, something caused the curtain inside God's Great House to tear completely into two parts. It tore from the top to the other end. God caused the ground to move about and the rocks broke. 52 God opened up the places where people had buried dead bodies. Many of God's people who had died became alive again. 53 They came out of those places after Jesus became alive again. They went into Jerusalem city and many people saw them.

54 The officer and the soldiers were still watching Jesus. They all saw the ground moving. And they saw the rocks breaking. They were very frightened and they said, 'It is true that this man really was the Son of God.'

55 There were also many women there. They were watching a short way from the cross* and they saw all these things happen. They had come from Galilee with Jesus to help prepare food for him. 56 Mary from Magdala was there. Mary, the mother of James and Joses, and Mary, the mother of Zebedee's sons, were also there.

Joseph from Arimathea buries Jesus' body

57 That evening a rich man who came from a town called Arimathea went to Pilate. The man's name was Joseph, and he had become a disciple* of Jesus. 58 Joseph said to Pilate, 'I would like to take the dead body of Jesus.' Pilate said to his soldiers, 'Give the dead body of Jesus to Joseph.' 59 So Joseph took the body of Jesus. He put a clean piece of soft white cloth round it. 60 And he buried the body in a large hole in a rock. He had made the hole to bury his own body when he died. After he buried Jesus' body, he put a very big stone across the hole to shut it. Then he went away. 61 Mary from Magdala and Mary, the mother of James, were there and they were watching.

They were sitting outside the hole in the rock where Joseph had buried Jesus.

Soldiers watch the place where Joseph had buried Jesus

62 The next day was the Sabbath* day. The leaders of the priests* and the Pharisees* met together with Pilate. 63 'Sir', they said, 'that man tried to cause people to believe things that are not true. He said, "I will come back three days after I die." He said that he would be alive again. We remember that. 64 Please would you put soldiers outside the rock where Joseph buried him? They should wait there for the next three days. Then his disciples* cannot come to take his body away from the hole. If they took the body away, then they could say to the people, "God has caused Jesus to become alive again." This will be the second thing that is not true. And it will be worse than the first thing.'

65 Pilate said to them all, 'You can take a group of soldiers to watch the place. Let them fix the rock well, so that no person can open it.' 66 So the leaders of the priests* and the Pharisees* went to the rock. They said to the group of soldiers, 'Watch this hole in the rock well. Do not let anyone go in.' Then they put a mark on the big stone. So, they would know if someone had moved it.

28

Jesus becomes alive again

1 Early, on the first day of the week, Mary from Magdala and Mary the mother of James got up early. They went to the hole in the rock where Joseph had buried the dead body of Jesus.

2 At that moment, the ground moved about. One of God's angels* came from heaven* and he went to the rock. He rolled the big stone away from outside the hole and then he sat on top of the big stone. 3 His face shone like lightning*. His clothes were very white like snow. 4 The soldiers who were watching

the stone in front of the rock were very frightened. They fell down on the ground like dead men. They were so frightened that they could not move.

5 Then the angel* said to the women, 'Do not be afraid. I know that you are looking for Jesus. The soldiers killed him on a cross*. 6 But Jesus is not here. He has become alive again. He said that this would happen to him. Come here. You can see the place where he was lying. 7 After you have seen that, you must go quickly to his disciples*. Tell them, "Jesus is alive again, and he is going to Galilee before you. You will see him there." That is the message that I have brought for you.'

8 So the women went away quickly from the hole in the rock. They were very frightened, but also very happy. They ran to tell the disciples* the angel's* message. 9 At that moment, Jesus met the two women. 'Hello', he said, and they went close to him. They held on to his feet and they said to him, 'You are so powerful. You are very important and beautiful.' 10 Then Jesus said to them, 'Do not be afraid. Go and speak to my disciples*. Say to them, "Brothers, Jesus says to you, 'Go to Galilee. You will see me there.' " '

The soldiers tell the leaders of the priests* what happened

11 The women went to tell the disciples* Jesus' message. Some of the soldiers who had watched the rock also went into the city. These soldiers told the leaders of the priests* everything that had happened at the rock. 12 The leaders of the priests* and the important Jews* met together. They talked about what they should do now. They decided to give the soldiers a lot of money so that they would obey them. 13 The leaders of the priests* and the important Jews* said to the soldiers, 'You must say this to the people. "Jesus disciples* came in the night and they took his body away. We were asleep when they did this." 14 If Pilate hears about this, we will explain things to him. He will know that you did not do anything wrong.'

15 The soldiers took the money. And they told the people, 'Jesus' disciples* took the body away from the hole.' The Jews* still believe that this really happened.

Jesus appears to his apostles*

16 After this, the 11 disciples* went to Galilee. They went to the mountain where Jesus had asked them to go. 17 When they arrived at the place, they saw Jesus. Then they went down on their knees. They told Jesus how powerful and beautiful and important he is. But some of his disciples* were not sure that it really was Jesus. 18 Jesus went close to them and he said to them, 'God has given me all authority. I have authority over everyone and everything. I have all authority in heaven* and in this world. 19 Go to the people in every country. Teach them how to become my disciples*. Baptise* them by the authority of God the Father, his Son and the Holy Spirit*. 20 Teach them to obey everything that I have taught you. You can be sure that I will be with you always. I will be with you until the end of time.'

WORD LIST

AD AD 50 means the year that was 50 years after Jesus came, and so on.

ancestors the people in a family who lived a long time ago.

angel a servant from God who brings his messages.

anxious, anxiety when a person has troubled thoughts.

apostle a special disciple* of Jesus. These men had a special job to do for him. Their job was to tell other people about Jesus.

baptise, baptism to put someone under water for a moment. They have done bad things. This shows God that they are sorry about all these bad things. Now they are going to obey God.

Baptist a man who baptises* people.

bridegroom a man who will soon marry.

care, take care of help someone who cannot help himself; do the good things that someone or something needs.

Christ The Jews* were waiting for God to send a special person to them. They called this person the Messiah. God had promised to send him. It means the person whom God sent to save people from punishment*. He would also be the king of the Jews*. He is the only person who can put us right with God. In the Greek* language, the special person was called Christ.

cross two pieces of wood fixed together.

desert a desert is a very dry place. Often there is a lot of sand and stones. There are not many plants. Not many people live there.

devil another name for Satan*.

disciple a person who wants to do the same things as another person, and learn from him; a person who agrees with Jesus; a person who does what Jesus teaches.

donkey an animal like a small horse.

fig a fruit that is good to eat.

forgive, forgiven to show love and not remember bad things against someone. When God does not remember the wrong things that we do. He chooses to do this.

God's Great House the special big house in Jerusalem. The people met there to pray.

grapes a fruit that people eat or make into wine*.

Greek the language that people from Greece speak.

hate not like or love.

heaven the place where God and Christ rule; the future home of the people who know God; the place where people will always be happy and without troubles.

Hell a place where people are not happy; a place where people who do not know God go after death.

Holy Spirit the name of one of the 3 persons who are God. He helps Christians to be more like God. We cannot see him. He makes people strong in their spirits*.

hypocrites these people say that they do one thing. But really they do something different. They want people to think that they are good. But really they are bad people.

Israel all the people in the families of Abraham, Isaac and Jacob. God chose Israel to be his special people. The word can also mean the country that God gave to these people.

Jew, Jewish a person that is born from Abraham, Isaac and Jacob and their children.

judge a person with authority to say if another person is right or wrong.

judge to say what is right or wrong, good or bad.

justice what is right and fair.

kingdom the people and places that a king rules are his kingdom. The people that God rules are his kingdom. They are the Kingdom of God.

lamp a light to use when it is dark; people burned oil in a dish to make a light; they called this a lamp.

laugh at to laugh against someone.

Law the Law of the Jewish* people. God gave the Law to Moses for his people to obey.

laws the rulers of countries make rules that people must obey.

lightning bright light that shines quickly in a storm, before a loud noise.

Lord someone whom we obey; a name for God or for Jesus.

needle a thin sharp piece of metal. It has a small hole at one end.

net people tie thin ropes* together to make nets. People use nets to catch fish or birds.

olive a tree that has fruit on it called olives. People make oil from olives.

Passover an important holiday for the Jews*. They eat a special meal on this day every year. They remember that God took them away from Egypt. They were slaves in Egypt and Moses led them away.

Pharisees a group of Jews*. Pharisees went to a special school to learn God's Laws*. They thought that they obeyed all God's rules. They did not like the things that Jesus taught. They thought that they did not do any wrong things. So they thought that they were very important and clever.

priest a man that gave gifts and burned animals to God for the Jews*. A man that God chose to do things for him.

prophet a person that tells people messages from God; people that spoke for God a long time ago.

punish, punishment to cause someone pain because they have done wrong things.

Roman a person or thing from the city called Rome.

rooster a large male bird; it makes a loud noise, early in the morning.

rope a long thin piece of material; strong material that people use to tie things together.

Sabbath the day when the Jews* rested. They did no work.

Sadducees a group of Jews* who did not believe in heaven*. They believed that dead people could not become alive again.

Samaria a part of the country called Israel*. It was between Galilee and Judea.

Samaritan a person who lived in Samaria*.

Satan the bad angel* that God sent away from heaven* a long time ago.

silver a valuable metal, but not as valuable as gold.

soil the top part of the ground. Plants grow in it.

soul the soul is a part of a person that we cannot see. Our soul is in us while we are alive. It lives on after we die.

spirit the part of a person that is alive, but which we cannot see. It can speak to other spirits and to the soul*. There are bad spirits and good spirits.

tax the money that people must pay to the Government. People gave their taxes to men who worked for the government. They then gave this money to their rulers.

trumpet thing which makes music, a loud noise; used to tell people to get ready for something.

vine a plant that grows a fruit called grapes*.

wheat a plant that has many seeds. Farmers grow wheat and people make bread with the seeds.

whip something used as a punishment* to hit someone who has done wrong things.

wine a drink made from grapes*. It has alcohol in it.

wineskin people kept wine* in wineskins after they had made it. These were like bottles and they made them from the skin of animals.

yeast people put yeast into flour and water to make bread. It grows in the bread. It makes the bread rise.